YORK FILM NOTES

Dracula
Director
Tod Browning

and

Bram Stoker's Dracula
Director
Francis Ford Coppola

Note by Brian Dunbar

Longman   York Press

York Press
322 Old Brompton Road, London SW5 9JH

Pearson Education Limited
Edinburgh Gate, Harlow, Essex CM20 2JE, United Kingdom
Associated companies, branches and representatives throughout
the world

Stills courtesy of Columbia Pictures
Screenplay printed by courtesy of Columbia Pictures

First published 2000

ISBN 0-582-43197-2

Designed by Vicki Pacey
Phototypeset by Gem Graphics, Trenance, Mawgan Porth, Cornwall
Colour reproduction and film output by Spectrum Colour
Printed in Malaysia, KVP

contents

author of this note Brian Dunbar teaches English and Film Studies at Lasswade High School Centre, Bonnyrigg, Midlothian. He also teaches film courses for the University of Edinburgh's Centre for Continuing Education, and is at present Director of Studies for its International Film Studies Summer School.

background

trailer

Mr. Browning is fortunate in having in the leading role in this eerie work, Bela Lugosi. What with Mr. Browning's imaginative direction and Mr. Lugosi's make-up and weird gestures, this picture succeeds to some extent in its grand guignol intentions. This picture can at least boast of being the best of the many mystery films.

The New York Times, 1931

Bela Lugosi gives a convincing performance and creates one of the most unique and powerful roles of the screen.

The Film Daily, 1931

The latest in a line of flesh-eating, blood-tasting anti-heroes which includes Hannibal Lecter and Max Cady, Coppola's Dracula is the most baroque incarnation yet of this *fin de siecle* phenomenon.

Pam Cook, Sight and Sound, February 1992

Whether you drink in Coppola's vision of Bram Stoker's novel as an erotic epic or are merely diverted by it as an extravagantly camp rock and roll through German Expressionism, decadent art, Cocteau and the wilder excesses of pantomime, what is indisputable is that the production design and photographic work make for sensational viewing.

Angie Errigo, Empire, February 1992

reading dracula

'I am ... Dracula.' These words have sent a shiver of excitement, fear and anticipation among cinemagoers for most of this century, instantly identifying one of the most famous icons in movie history. The influence of

reading dracula background

horror genre's most potent image

this fictional character has become all-pervasive: his image adorns breakfast cereals, toys, products of all kinds; he has become a cartoon character and a Marxist metaphor for capitalist greed, bleeding the populace dry. The name immediately conjures up images of fangs, cloaks, ruined castles, rapacious women and ... fear.

Above all else, the horror film relates to our fears: one of the few genres never to have gone out of fashion, because it addresses these fears, changing and adapting to reflect the concerns of succeeding generations, from Freudian preoccupations to economic and social changes.

The embodiment of our fears is the monster, and, of all the monsters, the vampire is the horror genre's most potent image. Films about vampires and Dracula in particular have been made in every decade since the 1930s.

Count Dracula, Lord of the Undead, is truly Undead since he has never gone away but endured a number of different incarnations according to changes in society. The white-haired mustachioed old man of Bram Stoker's novel had mutated by 1931 into a tail-coated, slick-haired foreign aristocrat, a 'lounge lizard' and seducer of women.

Variations on this image persisted, including the Hammer Films incarnation of the 1950s and 1960s with Christopher Lee as a more overtly sexual and dangerous vampire, and then in the 1990s Gary Oldman portrayed a more androgynous, animal-like creature in Francis Ford Coppola's version.

Whatever the incarnation, and they have as much to do with audience expectations and social attitudes as Bram Stoker, Dracula is both repulsive and attractive, terrifying and appealing. Outwardly, he is despised as a transgressor, an outsider who takes what he wants, a repellent, vicious, amoral being; but inwardly we admire him as a liberating force, someone who represents our yearning to be free of the restrictions of society, particularly in matters of sex.

But even where sex is concerned he is a contradiction. For women he is both their sexual liberator and the source of their punishment for attempted assertiveness and independence in the form of vampirism, which was from the early days of novel and film a symbol of disease, from syphilis to AIDS.

Even before the publication of the novel in 1897 the term 'vamp' had entered the language to describe a particular type of woman. By the time of the silent cinema the word had become very common and described a particular type of female character who embodied women's sexual freedom and who was, thus, a symbol of women's growing demands for social and sexual equality with men. For men, the horror of their women becoming vampires is also the horror of these same women's growing empowerment.

Dracula has become a symbol of evil, a sexual predator, an aristocratic foreigner, a rapacious capitalist, a carrier of sexual disease and diseases of the blood. But no matter how succeeding generations try to mould Dracula into an image more in keeping with their times, some things remain constant: xenophobia and the preoccupation with sex, and the empowerment of women.

The first film, *Nosferatu – A Symphony of Terror*, based on Bram Stoker's novel was an unauthorised version, made in Germany in 1921, by F.W. Murnau, and it presented a genuinely frightening vision of vampires. Thanks in part to the expressionist techniques in the film, borrowed later by Universal, the image of Dracula, as portrayed by Max Schreck, was totally different to Stoker's picture.

Count Orlok (the unauthorised film changed the names to try to avoid prosecution) is vermin-like, with a bald head, two fangs protruding from the centre of his mouth and with long twisted fingers. Truly repulsive, there is none of the magnetism and sexual attractiveness associated with later images of Dracula. The Dracula of Stoker's novel has this sexual element and attracts women, but in the film he was depicted as an old man with a large white moustache and a wisp of white hair around a bald head which was not an appealing image of a seducer for Hollywood.

It was not until an authorised stage version became very successful in the 1920s that the cinema's most enduring image of Dracula emerged. The actor playing Dracula on stage was cast in the role by Tod Browning and Carl Laemmle Jr for their Universal Pictures production of the stage play.

Initially Lon Chaney was selected for the part but died before filming began, leaving the film-makers with an alternative in the form of Bela

reading dracula

Lugosi. Hungarian by birth, Lugosi's heavily accented English, as well as his appearance – tail-coated evening wear, slicked back black hair and air of sophistication and urbanity – brought to the screen a presence of understated sexuality and exotic persona which was both dangerous and appealing to the audiences of the time. It also probably owed a little to silent screen romantic lead Rudolph Valentino.

Bela Lugosi's representation has dominated all future images – the tails, accent, hair, and mannerisms. From films and TV to toys, cartoons and food snacks, his image, suitably watered down, has been ubiquitous. It is Lugosi who is most closely associated with the role, and later actors taking on the role have had to live in his shadow. While many have attempted to deviate from the Lugosi representation and bring something of themselves to the part, such is the influence of Lugosi's performance in creating an undying icon that he is always there, whether in the voice, the hair or the costume.

Christopher Lee's version for Hammer in 1958 kept most of the physical similarities, but made Dracula taller and the sexuality less subtle and more animal-like. It was not until Francis Ford Coppola filmed his version in 1992, *Bram Stoker's Dracula* (to give it its full US title and to distinguish it from the 1931 film) that a new image emerged, one tied more closely to the original sources – the novel, and the historical figure, Vlad Tepes, who was the inspiration for Stoker's novel.

Thus, a study of Dracula in the movies has to examine the Bela Lugosi version – *Dracula*, directed by Tod Browning, and a later version to see how the image has remained constant in many ways and also to see how it has changed, influenced by advances in film techniques and cultural changes in society. For that, the logical choice is Coppola's, for its success and resort to the original novel.

For all the obvious differences between them, there are also many similarities. One is the fact that they both talk to us about the nature of cinema. The Browning version came in the early years of sound and is a prime example of an early sound film: studio bound, little movement and dialogue-heavy.

Disadvantaged as it might have been, it is nevertheless the film credited as establishing what we consider to be the horror genre. Apart from Lugosi's performance, the work of cinematographer Karl Freund with its expressionist influences created a visual approach to horror which would influence future films for decades to come.

Coppola's film, on the other hand, celebrates a hundred years of both the novel and cinema: there are references to films and cinema styles over the past century. His attempt to film Bram Stoker's novel faithfully for the first time, despite the introduction of an historical Dracula and an additional love story, is distinguished by the attempt to bring a new interpretation of the King of the Vampires to a contemporary audience.

Where the films differ is in their industrial and institutional contexts, the advances in special effects, and the portrayal of Dracula. What Coppola has tried to do is re-invent Dracula for a contemporary audience grown over-familiar with the character and his generic idiosyncrasies. In addition to the change in Dracula's appearance, he is now firmly an historical character with the issues of sex and blood now linked firmly to AIDS. Changing demographics have seen the average age of audiences fall, hence the young age of the cast of Coppola's film as opposed to the 1931 film.

THE HORROR OF SEX

A fearful fascination with sex is a common preoccupation of Victorian fiction, and *Dracula* was not the first vampire novel to link vampirism and sexuality. An earlier novel, Sheridan le Fanu's *Carmilla* has, as central character, a female vampire who preys on young women.

In such a patriarchal society as that of the Victorians, vampires betray male fears of women's sexuality and the potential threat to their patriarchy. Both male and female vampires represent the uncontrolled libido, and to surrender to it or be seduced by it is to be doomed.

Jonathan Harker is a typical Victorian middle-class straight-laced gentleman whose fear of vampirism is really a fear of women's rampant sexuality. Women, in fiction at least, have been particularly vulnerable to the vampire's erotic appeal, and their punishment has reflected women's sexual repression down the centuries by males fearful of their loss of power.

Women, as represented by Lucy Westenra, were demanding the vote and a greater involvement in society. This type of 'new woman' was a threat to the patriarchy of the Victorian age, expressed in Lucy's sexual assertiveness with all its implications for the Victorian family and moral system.

The female vampire's aggressive sexuality is traditionally seen as the prerogative of the male. With vampirism, men are placed in a position of sexual passivity and victimisation, formerly the role of the female.

The distinction between the private and public spheres of life was a feature of bourgeois Victorian society. It is Dracula's inability to accept this distinction that evokes such horror for the bourgeoisie: he not only threatens the public sphere but the private sphere, too. It is significant that he attacks mainly women, and primarily in the bedroom.

The classic vampire scene is of a woman sleeping in her bed, unaware of the vampire leaning over her about to bite her on the neck, considered an erogenous zone. Once bitten, she is no longer the same – and neither is patriarchal society. Sexual liberation was but one step to full emancipation.

VAMPIRISM AND DISEASE

Since vampires have to be defeated and normality restored with respect to women and men's position in society, women have to be punished for their assertiveness. This takes the form of depicting vampirism as a disease for which there is no cure, only death. The Victorians associated the disease of syphilis with promiscuity and sexual licence, and in the novel and subsequent films, vampirism is depicted sexually – the biting of the neck – and is therefore a sexually-transmitted disease.

In the novel of 1897, vampirism was a thinly veiled reference to syphilis; in 1919's *Nosferatu*, the vampire carries plague. By the time we reach 1992, however, Bram Stoker's *Dracula* equates vampirism with AIDS and, unlike the rather chaste 1931 bites on the neck, Dracula has sexual intercourse with his female victims. The link between vampirism, sex and disease is now quite explicit.

classic vampire scene

Once bitten she is never the same –
and neither is patriarchal society

DRACULA AND ECONOMIC FEARS

Earlier in the century Marx had used the vampire metaphor to discuss the workings of capital: 'capitalism is dead labour which, vampire-like, lives only by sucking living labour, and lives the more, the more labour it sucks'.

Writers, such as Mike Cormack, have likened Dracula to a form of capitalism called monopoly capitalism which brooked no competition and which was a threat to the liberal capitalism of the bourgeoisie. To defend itself the bourgeoisie moved progressively away from free trade and individual freedom in the late nineteenth and early twentieth century, and developed instead an ideology of collectivism and economic tariffs.

Moreover, Dracula is not only an aristocrat, he is a foreigner. The bourgeoisie came to regard not the market itself, but the overseas' competition as a threat, and sought to defend itself through protectionist tariffs. Dracula represents this threat, and successful action against him has to be collective. In both 1931 and 1992, there are concerns about the economic situation and immigrants which surface in the films.

THE APPEAL OF DRACULA

Readers recognise that Dracula is attractive precisely because he represents the dark side of our own natures. Not only does the vampire speak to our sexual fears and fantasies, and our desires to be free of restraint and moral control, but he is able to personify the wider social, economic and cultural concerns which surface in different generations.

Dracula may be repulsive and recognisably evil and self-serving, but because we recognise our darkest desires in him we experience conflicting emotions on his demise. Logic and reason say he must die, but that side of us controlled by passion and emotion feels a twinge of regret when he does. A Freudian analysis would identify Dracula as pure *id*, that part of the subconscious which deals with primitive and base desires. The struggle between our subconscious desire, the *id*, and our reason and conscious, the ego and super-ego, is one we all undertake and one which is re-enacted in every Dracula film. Perhaps this is the real reason for the appeal of Dracula.

key players' biographies

DRACULA (1931) – DIRECTOR TOD BROWNING (1882–1962)

Browning's films, both in the silent era and in sound, reflect his lifelong preoccupation with the unusual, the macabre and bizarre. Browning had left home when a teenager to work in a carnival which helps to explain his fascination with the grotesque.

Having worked with D.W. Griffith on *Intolerance* (1916) he began directing, and in 1919 began a ten-year association with Lon Chaney, renowned as the man of a thousand faces, an actor already well-known for the ability to contort his face and body into grotesque shapes. Among Griffith's silent films, which demonstrate his preoccupation with grotesque and bizarre characters as well as sexual infidelity and neuroses, are *The Unholy Three* (1925) and *The Unknown* (1927).

Browning had intended to cast Chaney in his version of *Dracula* but, as mentioned, Chaney died before the film began shooting and Bela Lugosi was given the role. Critics have argued that the film reflects Browning's lack of interest in the project after Chaney's death. However, the flatness of the film probably owes as much to the restrictions placed on it by the primitive sound facilities and the stage origins as anything else.

Browning, however, can be considered as one of the most influential figures in the development of the horror genre, both in terms of the sexual undertones, and the look of Universal's horror films of the 1930s. Much influenced by the work of German expressionists, who saw the look of a film as expressing subjective emotions experienced by the characters, he borrowed their chiaroscuro visual style with its emphasis on delineated areas of light and shade.

BELA LUGOSI (1882–1956)

Hungarian-born Bela Lugosi is the screen's enduring image of Count Dracula. No matter who has played the part since, something of Lugosi remains, and it is he more than anyone else who has shaped succeeding generations' view of vampires. Lugosi had played the role in a highly successful stage-adaptation of the novel in the 1920s and brought his stage persona to the screen.

He never shook off this role – future parts tended to be vampire roles or other horror movies although he also famously refused the role of the Creature in James Whale's *Frankenstein* (1931). Towards the end of his career, Lugosi was cast in embarrassing spoof films of his greatest character, and his last film was in Ed Wood's *Plan Nine from Outer Space* (1959), infamous for being possibly the worst film ever made.

Lugosi was to have reprised his role as a vampire but died shortly after filming was begun and was replaced by someone who looked nothing like him. While the rest of Bela Lugosi's career did not live up to the first screen performance, he did become one of the most enduring cinematic icons of the century.

EDWARD VAN SLOAN (1881–1964)

Of Dutch origin like Van Helsing, Van Sloan had a reputation for playing authority figures, such as doctors, professors and other intellectuals. He reprised his Broadway role of Van Helsing for the 1931 film and went on to play authority figures in many other films, particularly horror movies.

CARL LAEMMLE JR (1928–1979)

Appointed Chief Executive at Universal Pictures on his twenty-first birthday by his father, his productions of *Dracula* and *Frankenstein* established Universal as the leading studio for horror, and instigated one of the most enduring genres in cinema.

The films revealed the influence of German expressionism which continued to have an influence over the horror films of the 1930s and 1940s. Laemmle's father, Carl Sr was of German origin and many German expatriates from the German film industry – particularly the UFA studios – gravitated to Universal, bringing with them the influence of expressionism.

KARL FREUND (1890–1967)

As a cinematographer in Germany in the 1920s, Freund established a reputation for his expressionist lighting, camera movement and angles, and was the leading cinematographer of Germany's expressionist period. Among his German films are *Variety*, *The Last Laugh*, *The Golem*, and Fritz Lang's *Metropolis* (1926).

In 1929, Freund emigrated to the United States where *Dracula* was his first film. By the 1930s, he was also directing films including *The Mummy* (1932). In the 1950s, Freund left film-making to work in television.

FRANCIS FORD COPPOLA (1939–)

Coppola's early association with Roger Corman introduced him to low-budget horror movies, and the intricacies of film-making. Corman gave Coppola his first chance at directing with the low-budget horror film *Dementia 13* (1963).

Bigger budget movies followed, including the traditional Hollywood musical *Finian's Rainbow* (1968), but flopped. Coppola's script-writing talents were rewarded with an Oscar for *Patton* (1972). He has sunk much of his own money into his own production company, American Zoetrope, which has caused him a great deal of financial problems over the years. In 1972 Coppola made *The Godfather*, considered one of the greatest American movies, and then the equally critically-acclaimed *The Godfather Part Two* (1974). This was followed in 1979 by one of his most memorable films, *Apocalypse Now!*.

JAMES V. HART

He began work on his first draft of *Dracula* in 1977. Among his credits, is writer, *Hook* (1991); co-writer, *Contact* (1997); producer and executive producer *Hook*, and co-producer with Francis Ford Coppola, *Frankenstein* (1994).

EIKO ISHIOKA

Japanese designer Ishioka is renowned worldwide for her inventive work in costume design. Among the projects she has worked on are Paul Shrader's *Mishima* (1985), the stage play *M. Butterfly*, and Faerie Tale Theater's *Rip Van Winkle* for TV (1984) where she first worked with Coppola.

MICHAEL BALLHAUS (1935–)

Born in Berlin, Ballhaus, like Freund before him, became one of German cinema's most accomplished cinematographers. He began working in the USA in the early 1980s and was nominated for an Oscar for *The Fabulous Baker Boys* (1989). He has worked with Martin Scorsese on a number of films, including *GoodFellas* (1990) and *The Age of Innocence* (1993).

ANTHONY HOPKINS (1937–)

In the late 1960s and early 1970s, Hopkins was one of the leading Shakespearean actors on the British stage. An appearance on Broadway in the play *Equus* led to TV and film roles. It was not until his Oscar-winning role as Hannibal Lecter in *The Silence of the Lambs* (1991) that Hopkins became a very sought-after actor, specialising in roles of authority.

GARY OLDMAN (1958–)

Oldman's first starring role as punk rock star in Alex Cox's *Sid and Nancy* (1986) established his credentials as an actor who specialises in playing outsiders and psychotics. This was followed by his portrayal of gay playwright Joe Orton in *Prick Up Your Ears* (1987). Other notable outsider and psychotic roles followed in *JFK* (as Lee Harvey Oswald) (1991), *State of Grace* (1990), *Rosencrantz and Guildenstern are Dead* (as Rosencrantz) (1990), *Leon* (1994), and *The Fifth Element* (1997).

WINONA RYDER (1971–)

Full name: Winona Laura Horowitz. Named after place of birth, Winona, Minnesota. Has been acting since she was fifteen years of age. Films include *Heathers* (1989), *Mermaids* (1990), *Edward Scissorhands* (1990), *Night on Earth* (1991), *Age of Innocence* (1993), *Little Women* (1994), *The Crucible* (1996), and *Alien: Resurrection* (1997).

KEANU REEVES (1964–)

Born in Beirut, Lebanon, Reeves has progressed from playing vacant teenagers as in *Bill and Ted's Excellent Adventure* (1989) to leading men in films such as *Point Break* (1991), *Speed* (1994), and *The Matrix* (1999).

director as auteur

Just as poets, novelists and artists are considered the authors of their work – auteurs – so in film there has been a tendency to seek an author for films: the person responsible for putting the film on screen. In truth, however, there is no one person. Unlike most other art forms, film is the product of the collaboration of many people – director, screenwriter, producer, actors, set designers and editors to name only a few. Also, in mainstream cinema, the film-makers may be working within a particular genre which will impose certain restrictions and expectations.

The term auteur owes its origins to young French film enthusiasts who wrote for the magazine *Cahiers du Cinema*, founded by Andre Bazin in the 1950s. People such as François Truffaut and Jean-Luc Goddard sought to elevate the US films they so loved to the same status as other art forms. And since, in these other forms, the status of the art rests principally with the author, artist or composer, they took the director as their authors. They named this theory *politique des auteurs*, which was Anglicised in the early 1960s by American film critic Andrew Sarris as the auteur theory.

It is, however, one of the ironies of film-making that the person responsible for the detailed plots and dialogue – the screenwriter – is not accorded the same status as in the theatre.

In film-making, the screenplay is only the beginning. It then has to be visualised – the work of the director who has the overall responsibility for transferring the screenplay to the screen – so this made the director the obvious person to be the auteur. Thus, in the pages of *Cahiers du Cinema*, it was directors, such as John Ford and Alfred Hitchcock, who became feted as auteurs.

However, not every director is an auteur: there are factors which militate against this, for example, studio influence, the demands of the genre, the stars and their images. Indeed, in the 1930s and 1940s, many Hollywood

overriding vision and control

studios had recognisable styles: MGM had its lush extravagant production values; Universal had its expressionist-influenced horror movies; and Warner Bros had harsh, gritty realism and social comment.

Also in the 1930s and 1940s, producers exerted great artistic influence. David O. Selznick is the auteur usually associated with *Gone With The Wind*, not the director, Victor Fleming.

In the last twenty years when the director as auteur has been used as a marketing device to sell films, producers such as Don Simpson, for example, *Top Gun* (1986), can be considered auteurs. Although Simpson did not direct any films, as producer he had control over all aspects of his films and was certainly the vision behind them. Nevertheless, the most commonly accepted person as auteur is the director, simply because his/her role of being in overall control over the film-making process allows for greater freedom and influence.

For directors such as John Ford with his Westerns and Alfred Hitchcock with his thrillers, the notion of auteur is not unreasonable since their films display a continuity of style and theme and purpose.

For a director to be considered as an auteur, therefore, it has to be shown that this person has the overriding vision and control to carry it out. If the person has a number of films to his/her credit, then one should also examine the films for preoccupations, themes and style to see if this vision is carried on from film to film. If so, then there is a greater likelihood that the director can be considered an auteur.

Of course, the collective, industrial nature of the film-making process, the star system and the reliance on genre, all work against the auteur theory. On the other hand, many directors choose to construct a team which will work together on a number of films.

In addition, a director-auteur will often choose very carefully the cinematographer for their films. Many great film-maker auteurs have had great cinematographers. For example, Charles Chaplin had Rollie Totheroh, D.W. Griffith had Billy Bitzer, Orson Welles had Gregg Toland who, arguably, is as much the author of *Citizen Kane* as Welles.

Toland taught the young Welles the art of film-making and also had to turn Welles's suggestions and requests about types of shots and lighting into reality. In *Citizen Kane*, too, the screenwriter Herman J. Mankiewicz is often considered as much the author of the film as Orson Welles.

By the beginning of the 1970s new approaches to film analysis, such as Marxism, semiology and structuralism which put the emphasis on film as text, caused the demise of the auteur theory although it has been rehabilitated with the post-structuralists. Nowadays, the director as auteur is seen as one who has the overriding vision and control. For many film critics and students, the director is a logical point of departure when beginning any study of a film's worth.

An examination of the work of both Tod Browning and Francis Coppola reveals that they have sufficient artistic control over their films to be considered auteurs. In addition, Coppola – through his company Zoetrope Studios – exercised control over the entire production, while Carl Laemmle Jr – as chief executive of Universal and *Dracula*'s producer – supervised the overall production, leaving Browning to concentrate on script and filming.

TOD BROWNING AS AUTEUR

The director of the 1931 *Dracula* had had a long career in the silent cinema, working in horror or 'creepy' films. Most of his films reveal a fascination with the grotesque and bizarre, and contain many visual effects. For ten years, he worked with the actor Lon Chaney who was also associated with these types of films.

According to contemporary sources, Browning often produced the final shooting script himself, regardless of whose name appeared on the credits. The control he exercised over his projects is indicated by the 1925 Lon Chaney vehicle *The Unholy Three* in which the title 'A Tod Browning Production' appears above the title of the film.

In Browning's films, the lead characters tend to be bizarre and often predatory outsiders. There is no doubt that the character of Count Dracula fits this description and, perhaps, indicates one reason why Browning was attracted to the project. Many of his films from the silent era also display sexual themes, such as infidelity and transgression, which reappear in *Dracula*.

His later films never had the success of *Dracula*, and his 1932 MGM film, *Freaks*, was actually banned for many years after Browning himself withdrew it after only a few months on release. This film of grotesque sideshow acts, featuring actually physically-deformed characters, was a sympathetic portrayal of the oppression that these unfortunates suffered at the hands of normal society. It was considered too shocking because Browning had used people with actual deformities, not actors.

Glimpses of this sympathy for outsiders and their problems can be seen in *Dracula*, but are never developed. Perhaps if Lon Chaney, his first choice for the role, had lived, there would have been a more obviously sympathetic portrayal since Chaney had played characters like that on numerous occasions. No doubt Dracula would have been more grotesque and less attractive.

Thus, when considering whether the film as the work of an auteur, the areas to consider are:

■ themes – do they reveal Browning's obsession with the grotesque, the unusual, outsiders, and sexual transgression?

■ style – does the film's style have features familiar from other Browning films, for example, use of lighting, expressionism?

■ characters – are any outsiders, physically or mentally deformed, mistreated by normal society?

FRANCIS FORD COPPOLA

The production company TriStar gave Coppola full creative freedom. Some dominant themes had already emerged in previous films: 1) the quest (*The Conversation, Apocalypse Now*); 2) the merging of the Old World and the New (*The Godfather*); 3) the hounding of the non-conformist (*Tucker*), and, related to this, sympathy for outsiders (*The Outsiders, Rumblefish, The Godfather*).

In addition to complete creative control, Coppola also had artistic input into James V. Hart's script and had worked on the design of the film where he provided reproductions of paintings by Gustav Klimt, Casper David Friedrich and others to give them an indication of what he wanted. (As well as working together on the final drafts, Hart has claimed that Coppola's film style influenced his writing of the script.) He also discussed at length the type of look he desired for the film, and if it is remembered that Coppola was producer of the film then his input was undoubtedly the primary influence on the film.

Another indicator of an auteur is the amount of control exercised in the choice of cast and crew. As well as having the last word on cast, Coppola also controlled the appointment of non-acting members of the crew: Eiko Ishioka the costume designer had worked with Coppola before, and Roman Coppola his son was special effects adviser. His father, Carmine, scored the music for many of Coppola's previous films, although he died the year before Bram Stoker's *Dracula* was made.

Just as with Browning, an examination of the film will indicate features that suggest Coppola as an auteur.

■ themes – does the film deal with Coppola's preoccupations mentioned above?

■ style – are there stylistic features associated with Coppola, for example cross-cutting montage sequences, heavily stylised shots, overt editing?

■ characters – are there outsiders in sympathetic roles?

SIGNIFICANCE

As the largest-grossing vampire movie of all time and as an example of the body of work by such a distinguished director as Francis Ford Coppola, *Bram Stoker's Dracula* is worth studying, as is, despite its drawbacks, *Dracula*.

Tod Browning's film established a new film genre, one based on supernatural horror, and married expressionist techniques with the narrative drive of Hollywood, creating a template for horror films which would be influential for decades to come. And, with Bela Lugosi's portrayal, a cinematic icon was created whose image and meaning extends far beyond the cinema screen.

narrative & form

classical narration

Film can be divided into two main forms: fiction and non-fiction. The vast majority are fiction or narrative films. Both *Dracula* and *Bram Stoker's Dracula* are examples of narrative films whose primary purpose is to tell a story.

According to David Bordwell, the main form of story-telling which emerged in the sound era after 1930 was Classical Narration, or Hollywood Narration after the US's dominance of world commercial cinema. This form of film-making has story-telling as the principal aim with all features subordinated to this.

Bordwell identifies a number of features which define Classical Narration. Narrative itself consists of plot and style, where plot refers to the order in which events are seen on screen, and style refers to the film techniques which put the plot on screen. Among the features of Classical Narration are:

NARRATIVE AS CAUSE AND EFFECT

The events on screen do not exist in isolation. Events interact and future events are influenced by previous events. This gives a linear structure to films where the events or actions of a particular character will affect future events or characters later on in the film. For example, in both *Dracula* and *Bram Stoker's Dracula*, the arrival of Dracula in London causes storms heralding the disruption he will bring.

In *Bram Stoker's Dracula*, a montage sequence involves scenes where Dracula's voyage to London creates a storm which is seen to disrupt the lives of the ship's crew; disrupts Mina and Lucy whose suppressed emotions are unleashed, culminating in a kiss; and, finally, disrupts the animals in the zoo where a white wolf escapes. The entire montage sequence is united by the thunderous musical score. The biting of Lucy also is seen as cause and effect in the way she changes and behaves afterwards.

CLEARLY DEFINED INDIVIDUALS

To make it more easy for the audience to identify and empathise with, characters on the screen should have readily identifiable character traits; and the course of the film should be determined by individual actions rather than, for example, social forces. Events are always portrayed in relation to their effect on the characters.

In addition, certain characters can have a function within the narrative, for example Van Helsing's function is to gather together the forces opposing Dracula and so defeat him through collective action. Harker's function is to represent the rather conservative, repressed Victorian bourgeois male, while Dracula himself, representing unrestrained base desires, functions to provide the means by which the same base instincts are unleashed in the female characters.

LIMITED STYLISTIC FEATURES

In Classical Narration, plot takes precedence over style. Film techniques are designed to be 'invisible': in other words they should convey information to the audience to help it follow and understand the plot, but not be intrusive.

Among the deliberately limited number of film techniques employed is continuity editing which was designed to facilitate the smooth unfolding of events. A typical set-up would be an establishing shot where the particular characters in a scene would be shown in relation to one another, followed by cuts to close-ups of the individuals as they conversed. In other words, a film should be able to involve an audience in the events on screen and make it easy for audiences to follow events and see connections between them.

In *Dracula*, a scene which demonstrates this is the first meeting of Dracula with Mina, Lucy, Harker and Seward. When Dracula is announced to them at the opera we have an establishing shot which places Dracula in relation to the other characters. From this long shot, the film cuts to close-ups as the characters have their discussion. All the shots are from the position that the audience would inhabit; none 'cross the line' and are shot from the opposite side, as this would – it was felt – cause confusion in the spectator since the characters would appear to be looking in the opposite direction.

CLASSICAL NARRATIVE RESOLUTION

With Classical Narration, plot strands have to resolved by the end of the film, relationships between characters resolved and equilibrium restored (see Narrative Resolution).

VERISIMILITUDE

Films had to present an 'illusion of reality' to audiences, and the above features all contributed to this, particularly the unobtrusive use of film techniques.

Classical Narration had its heyday between 1930 and 1949. It had practical advantages as it made for quick and efficient film-making in an era when cinema-going was the dominant form of entertainment and studios were making movies in vast numbers.

However, by 1950, changes such as the break-up of vertical integration whereby the studios not only controlled the production of films but, through their parent companies, also controlled the distribution networks and cinema chains, plus the emergence of other forms of mass entertainment such as television, and the growing power of star actors, caused this system of film-making to begin to change. In its classical form, though, Classical Narration continued to dominate until the early 1960s.

DRACULA V. BRAM STOKER'S DRACULA

To varying degrees, both films display features of Classical Narration. Browning's film was made at the beginning of the sound era and when the features of Classical Narration were being established, although many had already existed in the silent cinema. This 1931 version is almost a textbook example of Classical Narration in terms of its structure, resolution, use of continuity editing and limited use of stylistic features.

By the time of Coppola's film in 1992, Hollywood had become increasingly concerned with style and special effects to appeal to an increasingly cine-literate audience and one which, through rock videos and MTV, had become used to more obvious stylistic features.

Technological advances also influenced the changes in film-making: the invention of the steadicam allowed greater freedom of movement for the camera and less reliance on editing to tell the story; special effects had advanced to such an extent that the use of computers could create virtually anything the director wanted.

Coppola's film is still primarily concerned with story-telling, but uses a greater number of stylistic techniques to do so – particularly in the camerawork and editing. The film still observes the rules of cause and effect and narrative resolution whereby the major problems of the main characters are resolved one way or another.

non-linear structures

As discussed above, all plots will have a linear structure in a cause-effect relationship but within this there may be other more general patterns dictated by other structural devices. A three-part structure has emerged in narrative films and other forms of story-telling, but other structuring devices can be found which are dictated by genre and theme.

While the principal structuring device is cause and effect – whereby every action has a reason and an effect on later events and the principal character is advanced toward a goal or goals – in narrative films this is often reduced to a simpler overall structure which can be described as:

■ equilibrium

■ disruption

■ restoration of equilibrium

This structure begins with an introduction to the main characters whose lives are disrupted by an event, for example a murder, the arrival of a particular character, etc. This creates problems which have to be resolved

non-linear structures narrative & form

before the end of the film, at which time, the disruption being eliminated, the characters can return to equilibrium.

The first part of the film is designed to inform us of the plot and introduce the main characters to us, as well as giving us any information which may be necessary to understand the characters' motivations and actions. In both *Dracula* and *Bram Stoker's Dracula*, the disruption is the arrival of Dracula in London, and equilibrium is restored on his death.

In Coppola's 1992 film, the structure also follows the equilibrium-disruption-equilibrium restored model, but the themes of love and redemption also structure the film. For Dracula, the disruption is the death of his wife and attack on the Church. Equilibrium is not restored until he is reunited with her at the end of the film. This is indicated by him changing to his original form as he dies in his wife's (Mina's) arms.

The 1992 vampire plot has the same disruption as Browning's film when Dracula arrives in London. This also returns to equilibrium when Dracula is defeated.

As a key scene in both films, the storm as Dracula arrives in England is used to symbolise the disruption he is about to create among the inhabitants of London as well as his ability to control nature. The deaths on the ship herald the disruption of normality for the characters in London and are a foretaste of what is to come. By controlling nature, the scene also signals the disruption of normality.

In Coppola's film, the storm also symbolises the beginnings of the release of sexual passion among the women. Not only is the storm at sea depicted, but, unlike Browning's film, the storm carries on to land where we see the effect of Dracula's imminent arrival on the wolves in the zoo, on Renfield at the Asylum, and, crucially, on Mina and Lucy. The storm now becomes a metaphor for uncontrolled lust, as seen later when Dracula, as monstrous wolf-like creature, has sex with Lucy.

GENRE AS STRUCTURING DEVICE

Within the three-part structure, more complex patterns can be constructed. Indeed, it is an indicator of genre that certain structures can be specific to particular genres. In addition, narrative resolutions are often genre-specific: Westerns tend towards shoot-outs, musicals often end on a big set-piece song-and-dance number, and horror movies have the monster confronted by the protagonist. This resolution symbolically represents us confronting our own fears.

THE COMPLEX DISCOVERY PLOT

Noel Carroll states that the horror film often uses a structure which he calls the discovery plot. This consists of three parts: onset; discovery; and confrontation. Some sub-genres, such as slasher movies and vampire films which include the two versions examined here, use a variation called the complex discovery plot which has four parts: onset; discovery; confirmation and confrontation. An examination of both films reveals that their structures conform to the complex discovery plot. In *Dracula* this is as follows:

onset: the introductory scene in Transylvania and Dracula's reintroduction in London (see Opening Sequences)

discovery: Van Helsing finds out about Dracula's presence and behaviour, and that he is a vampire

confirmation: at this point, it is the function of Van Helsing to convince the others, Seward and Harker, that the vampire really exists. This confirmation must happen before he can co-ordinate action against Dracula, for only collective action can defeat him. Thus, he must prove the existence of vampires in the face of sceptical resistance.

The confirmation part is an integral feature of the vampire film's structure. *Dracula* has a lot of expository detail aimed at an audience which had no intertextual knowledge to draw on. Cinematic vampire conventions were not stabilised until after this film which created them, therefore audiences were unfamiliar with conventions which, by 1992, would become over-familiar and clichéd to contemporary audiences.

While Coppola's film has expository scenes, these take up far less time and are dealt with brusquely as if assuming that modern audiences are very familiar with them. Indeed, the film takes time to inform the audience of a mistake concerning vampires: they cannot be killed by sunlight – their powers are weakened, but they can walk about in daylight. This misconception has been part of the vampire cinema lore since it was used to kill the vampire in *Nosferatu*, but Coppola's version is faithful to the novel.

confrontation: the forces to confront Dracula – Van Helsing and Harker – are gathered together and he is destroyed.

This narrative resolution is one of the defining features of the genre whereby there has to be a confrontation between the antagonist, in our case vampire, and the protagonist or the creature's nemesis. In vampire movies this is usually someone who is an expert in vampire-lore and so has the means to defeat him. For dramatic purposes, a confrontation is set up at some point in the film to anticipate the final confrontation at the end.

The first time they meet, its importance is conveyed through a series of close-ups from one to the other. In the 1931 *Dracula* Van Helsing uncovers the truth about Dracula when his reflection is not revealed in a mirror, a vampire trait. The second confrontation involves a battle of wits whereby Dracula tries to gain control of Van Helsing's mind but fails.

Both these confrontations have Van Helsing coming out the victor and dramatically serves to set up the final confrontation and our expectations of what will happen. This way of resolving the disruption of normality, created by the arrival of the monster, is universal in horror movies of all types and is one of the key ways in which the genre is defined. Any analysis of the structure of the films should examine the narrative resolutions of the films to see how the disruption is resolved and what similarities and differences there are.

opening sequences

An examination of the opening sequences will show the similarities and differences between the films. But it must be remembered that in 1931 there was no cinematic tradition of Dracula established, whereas in 1992 Coppola knew that the character of Dracula and the conventions associated with him were widely known and extremely familiar to audiences. Therefore, the information given in the opening scenes will differ to take account of this. Nevertheless, the opening sequences set up the plot and introduced us to the main characters and themes.

THE 1931 DRACULA

The opening of this version betrays its place in the early days of sound, and its theatrical origins with a cast list in a form which would be familiar to audiences from theatre programmes. The actors are also called players, another reference to the theatre and commonly used in early sound films.

Although Bram Stoker's novel had enjoyed success since its publication in 1897, and the stage play had been very successful in London and on Broadway, audiences would not have been as familiar as modern audiences with vampires – particularly Dracula. Therefore, the opening scenes of the film not only establish the narrative and introduce leading characters, they also provide audiences with information surrounding vampires with which they would be unfamiliar. Coppola's 1992 film, however, assumes the audience's familiarity with the conventions of vampires and Dracula, and keeps this exposition to a minimum.

After the cast list, the film opens to reveal a coach careering along a mountain path in the midst of a barren landscape. Inside, the travellers – all locals except Renfield, a lawyer from London – immediately inform us of the dangers of the area and that it is Walpurgis Night, when the forces of evil are abroad.

The opening sequence also creates the appropriate atmosphere, almost dreamlike in its depiction of Transylvania. While the inhabitants of this land seem to have hardly changed in centuries, it is clear from the appearance of Renfield that the film-makers have updated the film from the late nineteenth century to the 1920s.

We learn why Renfield is there, and numerous comments and looks prepare us for the entrance of the Count. At the coaching station frightened villagers try to persuade Renfield to stay the night, but as he is determined to go to meet his ride to castle Dracula he is given a crucifix as protection.

The clash of costumes emphasises the clash between the past and the present, the clash between the supernatural and science, for who is more logical than a lawyer? Before he sets off, he – and we – are also informed of the ability of Dracula to change shape to a wolf or bat and to drink the blood of the living.

Thanks to the cinematography and lighting of Karl Freund, this is the most atmospheric and successful part of the film. The castle is a Gothic ruin. Dracula appears from the top of the steps while Renfield is at the foot. Right away, an atmosphere of dread and power is established, with Dracula photographed from low angle. His immaculate costume seems out of place amid the ruins, and the mood is further enhanced when Dracula walks through a spider's web without disturbing it, while Renfield quite obviously cannot. Thus, the castle and Dracula are established as in the realm of the supernatural. They have the power here while mortal men have none.

The spider's web also symbolises the trap for Renfield, emphasised by Dracula's line: 'A spider spinning his web for the unwary fly'.

A disappointment are Dracula's Brides who display little of the overt sensuality and lust that we have come to expect from vampire women. This may have had a lot to do with the censorship regulations in force at the time in America. Certainly, a Spanish-language version made afterwards on the same sets had much more erotic wives.

BRAM STOKER'S DRACULA

The prologue of the film presents us with a very different Dracula, someone much more at home in his surroundings than Lugosi in his evening wear ever was (see Style: Costume). Far from being seen as a supernatural being, what confronts us is a flesh-and-blood man, a lover-warrior and defender of Christianity. This is no sophisticated, suave nineteenth-century aristocrat, but a powerful East European medieval warlord who disposes of his enemies in the cruellest ways imaginable – impaling.

In this prologue, Coppola not only shows us the inspiration behind Stoker's creation but also tries to create a real person capable of both undying love and hatred. A man whose powerful will and emotions can bring him back from the dead to seek his lost love. This creation is undoubtedly necessary if the spectator is to become involved in the love story which, along with the origin of Dracula, is established here. Thus, the prologue sets in motion the intertwined themes of undying love and blood.

The opening shots reveal an historical Dracula, of the Order of the Dragon, fighting the Turks who are sweeping across Europe after the fall of Constantinople in 1462. This is revealed in a voice-over by Anthony Hopkins in the character of Van Helsing.

While the voice-over continues, the battle scenes and subsequent impalings are portrayed as a silhouette on a red background, introducing the theme of blood. Stylistically, this helps to distance the events from the rest of the film and also refers to pre-cinema shadow shows, the first of many references to cinema in the film. Dracula's armour – red and reminiscent of anatomical sketches complete with a helmet shaped like a wolf's head – informs us of the connections with blood and pain to come.

On return home, Dracula discovers that his wife, Elisabeta, played by Winona Ryder, has committed suicide, tricked into believing Dracula was dead. Infuriated at the Church's announcement that as a suicide her soul cannot be saved, Dracula attacks the large stone cross in his chapel, sticking his sword into it.

From that moment, the defender of Christianity becomes its sworn enemy. As blood pours from the cross to cover the chapel Dracula fills a chalice with blood and drinks it in an act reminiscent of the Christian communion. This is the first of a number of parallels with Christ and establishes Dracula as a Messiah figure. 'The blood is the life', he announces. As the blood floods everywhere, we see a pool of blood enveloping the dead Elisabeta, preparing us for later when Elisabeta will be reborn through Mina drinking Dracula's blood. He vows to come back from the dead and take revenge.

So the prologue sets in motion a number of plot strands: the quest for his lost love; the reason for the use of Christian symbols against him; and blood as a symbol of life and also corruption, the conduit along which he corrupts.

The connection of Mina and Elisabeta is established with the same actress playing the parts. The colour and designs of their dresses also establish the connection between them (see Style: Costume).

After the titles, the film reverts to a more familiar setting: nineteenth-century London where Jonathan Harker is preparing to journey to Transylvania to meet his client, Count Dracula. In terms of the narrative, this scene serves to set up the reason for Dracula coming to London, and through Harker introduces Mina as the object of Dracula's attentions.

Above all, it introduces us to Dracula himself. This is perhaps the most anticipated scene in the minds of the audience, familiar with versions of it from previous movies and the novel. As a famous iconic movie scene, it leaves Coppola with limited scope for interpretation. He does so by keeping in the lines which have become part of movie folklore while reinterpreting the image of the character, and still maintaining the required air of menace.

His character is no suave, debonair European aristocrat. Although Gary Oldman felt obliged to keep the heavy accent made famous by Lugosi, everything else has changed. In this incarnation, Dracula sports a large elaborate plaited white wig, and the hairy palms described in the novel. He wears a flowing red costume, all of which, with his pale appearance, gives him a strange inhuman look; and the colours – red and white – reflect the themes of blood and death.

As an eastern aristocrat, who would have been influenced by Byzantium and Turkey, his costume reflects this and also includes on it a design of a dragon to remind us of the historical Dracula, of the Order of the Dragon. Also, the costumes flows out behind him like a large pool of spreading blood, again giving hint of the main theme of the film. This Dracula is very old, an androgynous figure, unearthly almost, unnatural, and light years away from Lugosi's suave 'lounge lizard'.

When we first see him, it is as a shadow which the camera focuses on moving across the wall. A sudden cut to a medium close-up of Dracula startles us since he is not where we expect because of the shadow. It informs us that Dracula does not inhabit the normal world: all things around him become enveloped in a supernatural, magical existence.

This is reflected in the style of the movie as the film proceeds. Those parts which are in Transylvania and at Carfax Abbey, the domain of the vampire, are filmed in a more stylised way to the London and house scenes to contrast the normality and abnormality (see Style).

narrative resolution

Both films resolve the disruption caused by Dracula's arrival by having Van Helsing lead a confrontation with the vampire, but this is the only similarity between the two versions.

If we look at the 1931 film first, then to our eyes it is disappointing. The killing of Dracula by Van Helsing, which should be the climax of the film, happens off screen and is almost an afterthought to Jonathan Harker's rescue of Mina. In the 1992 film, by comparison, the death of Dracula is a suitable climax to the film, the result of a chase across Europe by Van Helsing, Mina, Harker, Seward and Quincey Morris, reminiscent of chases in Westerns, an idea reinforced by the attack by gypsies loyal to Dracula.

However, while the confrontation of Dracula and his death by Quincey Morris (who killed him in the novel) is acceptably bloody and on screen in the 1992 version, it seems to take up less time than its status leads us to expect. Instead more time is spent resolving the love and redemption plots, with Dracula finally – as he lies dying – reverting to the human form we saw at the beginning before he became a vampire.

theme as structuring device

In 1931, the film uses the theme of good versus evil as a structuring device. This involves not only a confrontation at the climax of the film (which happens, infuriatingly, off screen), but also necessitates that there are confrontations earlier on between the two protagonists, Dracula and Van Helsing. The first takes place when Dracula is introduced to Van Helsing and is revealed, through a trick with a mirror, to be a vampire. The second is when Dracula tries in vain to control Van Helsing's mind.

GOOD VERSUS EVIL

The unending battle between the forces of good and evil is literally the battle between light and darkness. In both *Dracula* and *Bram Stoker's Dracula*, the realms which Dracula inhabits are always in darkness or they are dominated by shadow whereas the everyday world is brightly and evenly lit.

Since the battle between good and evil is also the battle between normality and abnormality, between the present and past, between science and superstition, the sets contrast in terms of size, shape and manner of photography with Dracula's castle and Carfax Abbey filmed from more extreme angles.

The settings reinforce the oppositions, with the past depicted as ruins while the present is modern with contemporary furnishings (see Style: Sets); with the superstitions and ancient magic personified by peasants crossing themselves; and the use of herbs, such as wolf bane, to keep the vampire at bay, contrasted with the scenes of blood transfusion and the factual knowledge of Van Helsing.

The Manichaean struggle between good and evil is symbolised in these dramatic contrasts. A large part of the dramatic expectations of the audience is based on the oppositions brought about by the symbolic use of lighting and set, particularly with the association between Dracula's attacks and darkness. The fact that the modern rational world has to resort to the traditional ways of killing Dracula seems contradictory, but serves to keep our fears alive by not dismissing the supernatural as false.

LOVE AND REDEMPTION

Being twice as long as Browning's film, *Bram Stoker's Dracula* employs a greater variety of structuring devices: there is the love story itself – boy has girl, boy loses girl, boy wins girl again – which, in turn, takes the form of a quest structure where Dracula seeks his lost love then proceeds to courting the object of desire, winning her and running away only for tragedy to strike.

Dracula as an historical figure is another influence on structure as this involves letting us see what the historical character was like, hence the

A theme running through Bram Stoker's
Dracula is that of the clash between two
worlds – the old world of superstition and
the new world of science

prologue where we are given the background to him becoming a vampire, and the final scenes where he is reunited briefly with his wife Elisabeta in the form of Mina.

In Coppola's film, the themes of undying love and redemption were added to the story. By showing how Dracula's wife died and his subsequent rejection of God, we are prepared for the ending where he finds his lost love and is therefore redeemed. In addition, Coppola uses the structure of the quest to structure the love story in the film.

The most powerful theme, that of blood and disease, is revealed through the mise-en-scène, which we shall consider in the next section.

NARRATION

Not to be confused with the term used by Bordwell to describe particular film forms, narration also refers to information given to us by a character in a film in the form of a voice-over, for example, or in POV shots.

Dracula employs omniscient narration where the audience is privy to all information and nothing is withheld. Audiences have a godlike view of events. However, in *Bram Stoker's Dracula* the film attempts to follow the structure of the novel by having the main characters expound information in voice-overs representing their written, typed and dictated thoughts. This has the potential to give us multiple viewpoints, but the device is used more to inform us of narrative details: the spectator is still given a privileged position where omniscient narration dominates.

By trying to adapt the novel as faithfully as he could, Coppola uses the original structuring device of the novel, the multiple viewpoints, which also serves to emphasise the theme of a hundred years of cinema by highlighting the technological advances in communication. Each of the characters, Jonathan, Mina, Seward, uses a form of communication to convey plot and character details to us: Jonathan has a journal as befits his conservative, staid outlook; Seward has his phonograph cylinder and ticker-tape machine, since, as a doctor, he is abreast of latest developments; and Mina uses a typewriter, a simple way of informing us that she is a modern woman.

However, rather than allowing this device to give us constantly shifting viewpoints, as in the novel it seems to serve other functions, such as indicating a world on the verge of the twentieth century. This highlights another theme of Coppola: the clash between two worlds, the old world of superstition and the new world of science. And this theme is continued elsewhere, notably when Lucy is given a blood transfusion.

style

introduction

In this section, the styles of the films will be examined in relation to how they inform us of narrative and theme. Film style refers to film techniques, and with plot it makes up the ingredients of narrative. There are two main areas: editing and mise-en-scène.

Mise-en-scène controls what we see in each shot and how we see it, while editing links separate shots and sequences of shots into a coherent order according to the demands of the film and the director's purpose.

EDITING

Editing can control the temporal, spatial, graphic and rhythmic relations between shots. The most common edit in films is the cut which is a simple splice. However, edits such as fades and dissolves can indicate the passage of time between the two shots. Space can also be controlled by the juxtaposition of an exterior shot of a house, for example, with an interior of a room, the assumption being that the room is in the house shown previously.

Also graphic similarities and differences between shots can be brought to the audience's attention. Lastly, the pace of a film can be dictated by the editing – a sequence of rapid cuts injects excitement into a film while longer gaps between edits gives an air of calm.

Intercutting is a function of editing used by both Browning and Coppola. Browning utilises this to show how Dracula is preying on Mina while the men discuss whether Dracula exists or not. Coppola uses it in a key sequence, uniting Mina's marriage to Jonathan and Dracula's brutal seduction of Lucy.

MISE-EN-SCÈNE

This refers to costumes, use of black-and-white or colour, set design and special effects, cinematography, and lighting. As we shall see, the two films differ widely in their application of film techniques.

dracula & bram stoker's dracula

To modern audiences, Tod Browning's *Dracula* is disappointing: it seems set bound and static with an over-reliance on dialogue. And the special effects, like wire for flying bats, create laughter rather than fear. On the other hand, Coppola's film could be said to suffer from stylistic excess covering every area of the film from costume to colour, tone to editing. However, we have to see the films in their historical and institutional contexts to establish the influences which led to their widely differing styles.

There are four main influences on the film's style:

■ Source material

■ Technological advances

■ Cinema

■ Genre

and all these will be examined in the Contexts section.

However, the source of material played a significant factor in the style of the films. Because Tod Browning based the film on the successful stage play, and because it was made during the early days of sound, his film has a static quality with few locations, and, except for a few key scenes, dialogue dominates the visual image.

Coppola, on the other hand, avoided the limitations and restrictions of the stage version by using the original novel which allowed him more of a free rein. In addition, he borrowed the structural device of the multiple viewpoint.

Also, by the time of Coppola's film, there had been great technological advances, and there were none of the limitations placed on Browning by primitive sound equipment. In 1931, colour was rarely used and still primitive, while in 1992 colour was used to great effect in Coppola's movie to define character, create mood, and to convey theme (see Colour in *Bram Stoker's Dracula*).

Cinema itself is the third influence on both movies: by 1931, many German directors and technicians were working in Hollywood and brought with them the influence of German expressionism (see Contexts: Technological advances) which attempted to convey subjective experience through sets and lighting.

Ideal for horror movies, the 1992 film also betrays the influence of German expressionism, as well as that of many films and film-makers in movie history. Since the novel was published almost at the same time as the birth of the cinema, Coppola took the opportunity to pay tribute to a hundred years of cinema by including references as homage to great moments of cinema in the past. There is more on this later.

This approach drives many of the stylistic features of the film, including the use of antiquated edits such as the iris, and the use of lap dissolves with maps to indicate journeys, a technique popular in the 1930s and 1940s.

Lastly, one should not forget generic influences: in this respect the films could not be more different. In 1931, the conventions of the genre, and the vampire movie in particular, were still fluid. In 1992, however, Coppola, had to work with the expectations of an audience which was very familiar, if not bored, with the conventions.

Audiences had, however, come to expect horror films to be more about gore and revulsion than shock, and were accustomed to seeing far more explicit scenes of violence than were allowed in 1931. (The same limitations also applied to how sex was depicted on the screen in 1931 – see Contexts: Censorship and Codes of Conduct.)

NORMALITY VERSUS ABNORMALITY

Both films deliberately attempt to highlight the disruption of normality with the abnormal arrival of Dracula. This is done by stressing the normal look of the London scenes and using more evocative styles for those scenes where Dracula dominates and controls. Dracula as an Undead is master of his environment. The normal laws of physics and nature do not apply. For this reason, both films attempt to convey this by employing particular stylistic effects.

In Browning's film, this is achieved through the lighting and set design: Karl Freund's expressionistic lighting creates an unworldly feel to the scenes in Transylvania and Carfax Abbey, in conjunction with the Gothic sets where huge arches and winding staircases loom over the characters, creating an atmosphere of foreboding and menace.

In the London scenes, particularly at Hillingham Asylum (ironically!) the lighting is much more evenly spread and brightly lit, suggestive of a normal contemporary society. Shades, props and walls are much lighter in shade emphasising the difference even more. Sets in London do not dwarf the characters. The overall effect is to associate the world of the vampire with the past and the supernatural while the London scenes are very much of the present and belong to the world of reason and science.

While also emphasising the dichotomy between the world of the vampire and the modern world, Coppola not only uses lighting and sets like the 1931 film to create the effect, but utilises camera techniques – such as extreme low and high angles – and special effects to suggest that Dracula belongs to a different dimension where natural laws do not work in the same way.

Therefore, in Castle Dracula, shadows seem to have a life of their own as Dracula is master of the dark. When Harker arrives at the castle, it is Dracula's shadow which appears first to him; later it appears from the other side of the shot from Dracula, creating unease and shock in Harker; when they discuss Dracula's acquisitions the shadow spreads menacingly over a map of London while Dracula himself makes no such movements; and, lastly, once Dracula is aware of Mina and her resemblance to his lost love Elisabeta the shadow seems to be about to attack Harker.

By contrast, the normality of the London scenes at Hillingham Estate and at Harker's firm of solicitors, are photographed in bright even lighting and angled straight on to emphasise the ordinariness of them.

sequential editing

EDITING

Browning uses straightforward sequential editing to propel the narrative, moving the audience from one event and location to another, only occasionally employing the editing to invite the audience to draw comparisons and conclusions between shots.

Cause-effect relationships are established through the editing. For example, after Lucy is bitten as she sleeps by Dracula there is a dissolve to a hospital operating theatre where Lucy lies dead after a failed blood transfusion.

Browning also employs intercutting to create tension and make the audience privy to information that the characters do not have. When Van Helsing is attempting to explain to Harker and Seward about the existence of vampires, the scene cuts to Mina leaving the sanatorium to meet with Dracula who envelops her with his cloak. There is then a cut back to the library where Van Helsing is still explaining. The intercutting allows us to see that Mina is in danger while the men discuss whether any danger actually exists.

Especially effective is the scene where Van Helsing, Doctor Seward and Harker are examining Mina's neck and wondering what might have caused the marks. The arrival of Dracula, announced by the maid, makes it clear to the audience who is to blame.

Editing in *Bram Stoker's Dracula*: Coppola's film is much more complex in the way it uses editing. As well as the basic uses of sequential and continuity editing the film uses editing techniques such as the iris and lap dissolves. Both cinema and the original novel emerged about the same time: the late 1890s.

The iris is used time and again in the film. When Jonathan Harker says farewell to Mina in the garden at Hillingham Estate, the camera moves in on one of the peacocks roaming around. The eye of its feather becomes a train tunnel as Harker begins his journey to Transylvania. This shot is the first of many involving eyes, mainly dissolves, which symbolise Dracula's brooding presence and awareness of everything.

Lap dissolves are not only used to shift time and place, but also to create connections between characters and allow the spectator to be aware of future narrative developments. One can see the film as a love story, indeed a love triangle, where Dracula and Jonathan Harker compete for Mina's affections.

To emphasise this narrative element and prepare the audience for this struggle, Coppola employs the lap dissolve to establish this when Harker meets Dracula. Lying on the table is a photograph of Mina. As Harker and the Count talk, the photograph is superimposed between them anticipating the struggle for her love which will emerge later.

MONTAGE

Montage sequences are employed to far greater effect in Coppola's film than in Browning's. Indeed montage is seen as a stylistic trademark of Coppola, in particular in the celebrated sequence in *The Godfather* where Coppola intercuts the baptism of Michael Corleone's nephew with the massacre of the Corleone's enemies. Coppola uses montage not simply as intercutting to show events happening simultaneously, but also to compare and contrast, and to invite the audience to comment on what is seen.

In *Bram Stoker's Dracula*, Coppola again uses a wedding scene as part of a montage sequence to contrast the brutal attack on Lucy with Mina and Jonathan Harker's wedding in Transylvania. In a POV pixilated sequence, Dracula renders unconscious Holmwood and Morris who are protecting Lucy.

Then we cut to the wedding ceremony. The church, priests and wreaths on Mina and Harker's brows are all reminiscent of the opening sequence when Dracula renounced God, and of his wife Elisabeta reminding us of what he had lost and what he has found again in Mina.

Then we cut back to Lucy's room. There is a close-up of Dracula as an old man outside the window. He says, 'Your impotent men with their foolish spells cannot protect you'. Although addressed to Lucy, these words with their overtly sexual meaning obviously refer to Mina and her wedding. This is reinforced by cutting back to a close-up of Mina. By this point it is obvious that the attack on Lucy is in retaliation for, and in frustration at, Mina's wedding.

We cut back to Dracula condemning Lucy to 'living death, to eternal hunger for living blood', then cut to Harker and Mina drinking communion wine. The juxtaposition of these shots leaves us in no doubt that Dracula's lust for blood is a perversion of Christian symbolism.

Then we cut again to Dracula, now changing into a wolf, and then crashing through Lucy's window to attack her on the bed. We then cut back and forward between the attack on Lucy, and Mina and Harker kissing, contrasting the sensitivity of the wedding scene with the ravishing of Lucy. Finally, Lucy's room explodes in a tidal wave of blood before we cut to Mina and Harker kissing as the scene fades out.

The sequence unites several themes: Dracula's quest for his lost love; transmission of disease through blood; and vampirism equated with unrestrained sexual lust. It also reminds us that Dracula is essentially evil.

LIGHTING AND CINEMATOGRAPHY

Karl Freund's expressionist lighting is the defining stylistic element in the 1931 film. Allied to the composition of his shots and Gothic sets, he creates a huge brooding expanse that is the entrance to Dracula's castle which immediately conjures up the appropriate creepy atmosphere.

Browning prepares us for Dracula's entrance by filming Renfield in long shot, making him small and insignificant, and dwarfed by the huge staircase and the Gothic ruins of Castle Dracula.

Freund's lighting gives us the impression of a vast sombre cathedral belonging to another time. When Dracula enters, he is dressed in the familiar evening attire with his cloak raised towards his face. The camera stays on Dracula as he makes his way down the staircase heightening the drama and expectations of his entrance.

To add to the air of unreality, as previously mentioned, Dracula walks through a cobweb without disturbing it. This effect is achieved very simply but effectively by employing a match on action, cutting when Dracula approaches the cobweb, and in the next shot showing him on the other side. The fact that Renfield has to hack through the cobweb indicates Dracula's control of this realm.

Throughout the film, Freund uses close-ups sparingly, and almost all are of Dracula's face – his eyes highlighted from the surrounding darkness to emphasise his hypnotic powers and sexual magnetism. It is almost always women who succumb to this shot.

With the exception of a few conspicuously stylised sequences – in particular, the shadow of the dead captain of *The Vesta* lashed to the wheel, reminiscent of *Nosferatu* – little of the rest of the film lives up to the opening. The dead captain scene, and other shots such as those of Lucy after she has become 'the bloofer lady' prowling in the park edges, are all scattered between long dialogue sequences staged in medium and medium close shot.

COSTUME

Browning's film betrays its theatrical origins in the costumes which have been updated to the contemporary society of the 1920-30s. Male characters' costumes are functional: Renfield's clothes in Transylvania indicate he is an outsider and possibly, given his briefcase, in a profession such as law. Van Helsing is first seen with a white coat indicating his medical status, while Dracula himself goes through the entire film dressed for a night at the opera. However, when Mina has been bitten and infected her costume change has a narrative purpose: the silky, slinky evening gown denotes her change of character to a more aggressive sexuality.

Costumes and make-up in *Bram Stoker's Dracula*: Designer Eiko Ishioka was given a free hand to express the appropriate mood for the film through the costumes of the characters. With one exception, Coppola had gone for a young attractive cast which he felt would allow him to use costumes to create a striking effect, and establish mood, period and characters.

As well as the designs, the colours were significant. Dracula was given the colour of scarlet, white, black and gold. Mina's inexperience and naivete were signalled by green, while Lucy was given orange, perhaps to indicate a sexual awakening, but not yet the red associated with the vampire's blood-lust and sexual desire. Jonathan Harker wears black and other dark

Mina is soon to become a vampire

Mina (Winona Ryder) is seduced by
Dracula's (Gary Oldman) eternal charms
in *Bram Stoker's Dracula*

muted colours to emphasise his stiff, bourgeois, conservative image. Quincey Morris, the Texan, is typically American with cowboy boots and Western-style jacket and Stetson.

The colour red is unique to Dracula, save for the absinthe scene when Mina is being seduced by Dracula. Here, she wears red signalling her lust for Dracula and the fact that she is soon to become a vampire.

As well as colours, the designs of the costumes were intended to be significant. The colour and designs on Elisabeta's dress, for example, are similar to those on Mina's. Both have patterns of leaves, suggestive of nature and natural order, while Lucy's has snakes representing the biblical associations of sin and lust.

As an extrovert and, to a certain extent, eccentric character, Lucy's costumes had to reflect these aspects and be sexy and unique with an aristocratic elegance. Lucy's elaborate white wedding dress was, therefore, modelled on the Australian frilled lizard, again reinforcing the reptilian connections.

When she becomes a vampire and satiated with blood, the frilled collar conveys a swollen appearance and an unnaturalness which indicates she is no longer human. The white colour of the material, contrasting with the blood around her mouth, gives a truly alien appearance.

However, it is Dracula who has the most elaborate costumes and changes of appearance. There are a number of incarnations: the historical soldier; the old wizened boyar; the werewolf creature; the Byzantine figure; and the young dandy in London.

Ishioka designed the man-beast armour which we see Dracula wearing in the prologue. This costume foreshadows the change in Dracula from man to vampire and shape-changer, and establishes the vampire's association with – and control over – wolves. The armour itself is heavily stylised, giving the effect of anatomy drawings of muscles with the skin removed. The helmet is similarly styled, but in the shape of a wolf's head. The overall effect is to create a more than human warrior inextricably associated with pain and death.

The designs of Dracula's costumes were intended to emphasise his androgynous quality. He is a complex character who has many sides mentally and physically. His true self is not easily revealed, and we are unsure whether he is male, female, animal, devil or angel. At times he appears to be an incredibly ancient Byzantine or Turkish figure; at other times, in London, he is a young, attractive, fashionable, exotic dandy whose clothes suggest the traditional evening wear restyled by Armani.

colour in bram stoker's dracula

Although colour has been discussed above as a part of costumes, one particular colour – scarlet – so dominates the film that it deserves a section to itself. The film is drenched in blood, and blood is the primary metaphor in the film: it is the blood of the historical Dracula's victims; it is the blood that the vampire needs to survive; it is the blood sacrament between God and man; it represents diseases, such as AIDS, carried in the blood; and also symbolises decadence.

From the opening shots of Vlad Tepes's battle against the Turks against a blood-red sky, followed by the renunciation scene where his private chapel literally flows with blood, the link between blood and Dracula is established.

When Vlad Tepes renounces God for condemning her to damnation for her suicide, he drinks the blood he has caused to flow from the religious artifacts as a perversion of the Christian communion. Like Christ, Dracula offers eternal life through the drinking of his blood, as Mina does. The act of drinking his blood is performed at the end of their love-making and is clearly associated with the sex act:

```
MINA
        You are my love - and my life. Always -
He enfolds her, bends her backward gently.
```

DRACULA

> then — I give you life eternal. Everlasting
> love. The power of the storm. And the beasts
> of the earth. Walk with me — to be my loving
> wife ... forever.

MINA

> Yes — I will — yes —

Wider shot.

Dracula caresses her face as tenderly as a child.
She is willing. She is ready. He gently turns her,
exposing her neck, kissing her softly.

DRACULA

> I take you as my eternal bride —

She moans in ecstasy — a tiny grimace of pain as he
enters her veins.

Close-up — his chest.

With his long thumbnail, he opens a vein over his
heart. We see his beating heart.

DRACULA

> — flesh of my flesh — blood of my blood ...
> Mina ... Drink and join me in eternal life —

He pulls her submissively to his chest. She drinks.
She swoons as his life runs into her.

Reverse angle on Dracula.

He falters — tears welling up — suddenly fighting
his desire. He shoves her back in anguish.

DRACULA

> I cannot let this be!

MINA

> Please — I don't care — make me yours.

colour

symbolist movement

DRACULA

> You will be cursed — as I am — to walk in the
> shadow of death for all eternity. I love you
> too much — to condemn you!

She shudders – pleading, holding him, caressing him.

MINA

> Take me away from all this death!

*She forces her lips back to his chest. His moans of
ecstasy build to a climax; then he wraps her in his
arms, holds her close.*

As well as containing obvious references to Christian ritual and eternal life, the intimacy of the scene is very touching and is clearly designed to produce sympathy for a vampire who is actually unwilling to create another victim. Dracula's feelings for Mina contrast with the montage sequence when, in response to the marriage of Mina and Jonathan, he sexually attacks Lucy, turning her into a vampire.

Their love-making – and Mina's desire to be a vampire out of love for her prince – is foregrounded in the Rules's Café scene where she drinks absinthe and wears a red dress. As red is Dracula's colour, on Mina it symbolises that she is soon to become a vampire.

In the Symbolist movement of the late nineteenth century, red is seen as the colour of decadence, just as absinthe was considered the drink of decadence. Symbolism was a late nineteenth-century art movement which drew upon myth, fantasy and historical references. It was an aesthetic reaction to the growing power of science and industry; an erotic rebellion against the mannered behaviour of the bourgeoisie.

Symbolist artists took as their inspiration images from dreams and the unconscious. Escape was sought in dreams through drug-taking or drinking absinthe. Individual images in the film which are clearly inspired by symbolism, include Hillingham crypt and Dracula's castle, the Brides' flowing hair and Lucy's ethereal but erotic look as the vampire's willing victim.

The connection between vampirism, sex and disease is highlighted through the imagery to make metaphorical comment on the AIDS epidemic, and the parallels between AIDS, sex and death, and vampirism, sex and death, 'a disease of the blood unknown', as Van Helsing says.

Lucy and Mina are then condemned when they exchange 'precious bodily fluids' with the vampire. When Van Helsing talks to his students about 'the diseases of Venus' or venereal disease the implication is not just that it is associated with sex; it is also associated with women.

Van Helsing even asks Harker if he had tasted of the blood of the vampire women. The outstanding impression given is that it is a disease associated with increased female sexual activity. This hypocrisy perfectly fits the Victorian attitude to sex – full of suppressed emotion and longing, as exemplified in Jonathan Harker.

The dreamlike sequence where Harker is raped by Dracula's Brides illustrates how vampirism is about hidden desires. The Brides' attack on Harker is explicitly sexual, and represents the suppressed desires he and other Victorians felt they had to keep in check, or at least save for the brothel, out of the way of polite society.

sets

CASTLE DRACULA

For both films, the sets play an important part in creating the appropriate mood, particularly that of Dracula's castle, set amid a blasted barren landscape where nothing lives, a lifeless place fitting for its inhabitant.

In keeping with the dichotomy between normality and abnormality, with the past representing abnormality, Coppola had the castle built as a part-ruin, but visualising Dracula as someone who would be in touch with the latest scientific developments, he had the castle depicted as if it were undergoing repair, with steel scaffolding on it. This also reminds us of one of Coppola's preoccupations – the interaction between the old and the new.

The castle itself was inspired by a painting entitled 'Resistance – The Black Idol', by Frantisek Kupka. Its name and the shape of a seated brooding figure dominating the landscape perfectly suits the character of Dracula who first dominates Transylvania and then London.

The limited sets of the 1931 film once again betray its theatrical origins, while Coppola allows himself the luxury of a greater number. The asylum, in particular, is straight from a nightmare. With the 'nurses' wearing rectangular cages on their heads to protect them from the inmates, it is difficult to distinguish the sane from the insane.

The asylum is more reminiscent of bedlam than a modern mental institution, whereas the even lighting of the Hillingham estate, the framing of the shots, and the preponderance of straight lines and right angles, all reinforce the atmosphere of logic and reason which surrounds it. Only when Dracula arrives does this change, and canted shots are used to show the disruption of normality, and the eruption of the women's sexuality.

special effects

The films are quite different in their use of special effects, although a closer examination of the later film reveals that Coppola has adapted special-effects techniques used in the earlier days of film and has eschewed the latest computer techniques (see Contexts: Intertextuality).

In Browning's *Dracula*, the bats are quite obviously fluttering on wires and are laughable to our sophisticated senses. Much more effective is when Browning uses editing to suggest a transformation. Also used in the film are miniatures of ships and Dracula's castle, neither particularly effective, and a process shot of the coach careering through the Borgo Pass.

Perhaps the most telling special effect in Browning's film is when Karl Freund highlights Dracula's eyes by focusing light through two small holes in a piece of cardboard, to heighten the eerie effect.

For *Bram Stoker's Dracula*, Coppola wanted to use techniques which would hark back to the beginnings of cinema itself and the publication of the novel, and be as simple as possible. He also stated that he did not have the budget for sophisticated electronic and computer effects. Tricks included running the film in reverse: demonstrated when Lucy is writhing on her bed to give a strange unnatural look, and when, as a vampire, she is cornered in the crypt and climbs backwards into her coffin; multiple exposures, showing, for example, Harker's face and a train in the same shot; mirror effects, and effects suggested by other films, such as combining rear projection with live action as in the shot when Harker and Dracula are walking along the hallway in the castle.

The technique used to show the werewolf creature's POV in its attacks is called pixilation, which is akin to animation: the camera is prepared to take pictures frame by frame. The frames are then exposed erratically, perhaps one, then a short burst of several, then two, then one, etc. The overall effect is animal-like, almost alien and extremely threatening.

music

One of the features of *Dracula* that audiences notice almost immediately is the lack of background music. Apart from the opening and closing titles, the only place where music appears is when it appears to authenticate the characters' appearance at the opera.

This diegetic use of music was the only type used in films in the early sound era. Any background music, which did appear, was used during the transition from one scene to another. There are two main reasons why music, which was such an important part of the silent cinema, was not utilised right away.

The first is that the coming of sound added a further layer of reality to film: characters became more fully realised; sound effects, such as everyday noises, created a verisimilitude which audiences had not encountered before. Music, it was felt, would detract from this new reality and be intrusive for audiences. Within a few years, however, background scores were added to restore the emotional involvement which had been removed by its omission.

Another reason was the primitive technology available for sound recording and editing. In addition, the early sound-on-disc format for synchronising sound and image was virtually impossible to edit. The first sound-on-film system by Movietone had a twenty-frame (approximately one-second) gap between sound and picture, and editing resulted in continuity problems.

music

emotional intensity

Another system emerged in 1929 which separated the sound strip from the image, but it was not until 1932 that studios began recording music, speech and dialogue separately that the problem was fully overcome. One of the first films to show the possibilities of this new approach was *King Kong* (1933).

On the other hand, *Bram Stoker's Dracula* boasts a powerful operatic-like score overfull with emotional intensity. As well as a recurring motif that both signals Dracula and danger and foreboding, the score is used to highlight the intimate moments and growing intimacy between Dracula and Mina, and helps to create sympathy if not empathy for the vampire.

contexts

production history

DRACULA

In 1924, after six years of trying to find a writer to adapt Bram Stoker's novel, Hamilton Deane, a provincial play producer and actor, wrote one himself.

The original stage production of the play opened at the Grand Theatre, Derby, in 1924. After three successful years touring the provinces the play opened in London's West End at the Little Theatre. It was poorly received by the critics, but audiences loved it. Horace Liveright, a Jazz Age producer, entrepreneur and publisher, purchased the USA rights of Deane's play and hired John L. Balderston, a journalist, playwright and screenwriter, to adapt the show for its Broadway première.

Balderston got rid of the character Quincey Morris, and sharpened the conflict between Van Helsing and Dracula. It is Balderston's changes which eventually appeared in the Hollywood version. As in the play, the setting was kept as modern London, but updated from the 1890s to the late 1920s. Balderston also updated – and made sharper – the dialogue for American audiences. In three seasons, eighteen months, with several touring American companies, *Dracula* took 2.5 million dollars.

Universal's interest in *Dracula* began in spring 1927. Carl Laemmle ordered studio readers to review the novel and the play, a natural step since Hollywood likes adaptations of popular stage and literature because of the promise of a guaranteed audience. This was particularly true following the advent of sound. There was a mixed response from the readers. Some considered the story too gruesome. Nevertheless, *Dracula* went into pre-production, albeit rather slowly.

In August 1927, with *Dracula* in preproduction, Browning began work on *London After Midnight*. The plot of this film and book seems just too close for coincidence, the major difference being that the vampire turns out to be a hoax, the traditional way of handling supernatural themes before *Dracula*. The story was copyrighted just a few days before the American version of the play and released on 6 December, 1927. *Dracula*, the play, opened on 5 October, 1927, and *The Jazz Singer* on 6 October, 1927, heralding the arrival of the sound era.

In 1929, Carl Laemmle appointed his son, Carl Jr, Chief Executive at Universal when he turned twenty-one. By August 1930, Universal had finally acquired the rights to *Dracula* and assigned the writing of the screenplay to novelist Louis Bromfield whose treatment was based primarily on the book. Continuity writer Dudley Murphy was assigned to work with Bromfield to produce a workable script within the budget. However, probably due to financial pressures, when Browning and Garrett Fort were given the script to turn into the final screenplay they basically adapted the stage play.

Laemmle Jr ordered Dracula to be put into production with a budget of almost $400,000, an impressive sum given that half that amount was considered a good budget for an A-class vehicle, and even more so when you take into account the fact that the studio was in financial trouble at the time.

The original choice of director had been Paul Leni, another leading German expressionist director, and Conrad Veidt, who starred as the somnambulist Cesare in *The Cabinet of Doctor Caligari*. But when Leni died suddenly of blood poisoning in September 1929, Veidt – upset at his friend's death but also it is claimed unwilling to make talking pictures in English – left for Germany.

Browning, who, in 1927 was one of MGM's top directors, had tried unsuccessfully to gain the film rights for *Dracula*, was approached by Universal. He accepted and wanted his friend Lon Chaney to play Dracula. Carl Laemmle Jr agreed, but tragedy struck again when Lon Chaney died.

The part was then offered to Bela Lugosi who had made a success of the role on stage. Lugosi had previously been considered, but was passed over

production history

as not being sufficiently well known to audiences. Undoubtedly, this recasting was the single most important factor in the creation of Dracula as we know him.

Chaney's ability to play grotesques would have created a vampire that was closer to Stoker's creation and less sympathetic to audiences, but a trick of fate allowed Bela Lugosi to repeat his stage role, influenced by silent stars, such as Rudolph Valentino, and their 'sexual magnetism' – and his own heavily accented but sexually attractive English.

After years of political activism in his native Hungary, actor Bela Lugosi fled to the USA to continue his acting career. He jumped ship in New Orleans, later making his way to New York and its Hungarian theatre community. There, Lugosi won several parts in well-reviewed shows, starting with *The Red Poppy* which opened at the Greenwich Village Theatre in December 1922.

According to legend, his on-stage love-making was so passionate that he broke one of his co-star Estelle Winwood's ribs. She and Lugosi both verified and denied this tale.

Lugosi was given the *Dracula* stage role when British actor Raymond Huntly, who had played the role for four years in both Britain and America, turned down the role in the Broadway version of the re-written Balderston version of Deane's play.

And the rest is history. Lugosi went to Hollywood to repeat his stage triumph in the Universal Pictures version, directed by Tod Browning. After *Dracula*, Lugosi turned down the role of monster in *Frankenstein*, thus allowing Boris Karloff to come in and quickly eclipse him as a horror star.

After the early 1930s, Lugosi could only secure supporting roles at major studios, so chose to work as a star at independents such as Monogram, and in B movies. He continued to play the *Dracula* part on stage throughout the 1940s and early 1950s, but repeated the role only once on film, in the affectionate 1948 Abbott and Costello romp, *Abbott and Costello Meet Frankenstein*.

In the early 1950s, Lugosi had himself admitted for treatment for medically-induced drug addiction. Befriended by Ed Wood he made a number of dreadful movies for him, culminating in the terrible *Plan 9 from*

Outer Space, in which he appears only briefly, dying not too far into the production.

For the other parts in *Dracula*, Edward Van Sloan, Herbert Bunston and Dwight Frye reprised their stage roles of Van Helsing, Seward and Renfield respectively. For the romantic leads, Universal chose Helen Chandler and David Manners.

The final cost of *Dracula* was $441,984.90, with a Spanish version made alongside on the same sets.

The film was released on 12 February, 1931 and was an instant success. Coupled with the release and success of *Frankenstein* later in the year, *Dracula* helped to ensure Universal's reputation as the pre-eminent maker of horror films. More importantly, by combining Hollywood's narrative drive with German expressionism, it influenced the direction of horror up to and including Coppola's 1992 film.

It also gave the world not only an enduring screen icon, but a cultural icon as well. The film, therefore, has an historical significance which outweighs its artistic merits.

BACKGROUND TO BRAM STOKER'S DRACULA

A film version of *Dracula* was sought by Coppola as a commercial project which would pay off the debts he had incurred after the failure of his Zoetrope studios. He wanted to show the studios that he could deliver a big-budget mainstream film on time and within budget.

Winona Ryder had pulled out of *The Godfather Part III* and, anxious to make amends, she had brought Coppola some ideas including James V. Hart's script. Within four months, she had been cast as Mina, and Coppola and Hart were hard at work on an approach to the film and its aesthetics. Coppola liked the way the script stuck to the novel, but they agreed that a compelling theme was needed to engage audiences who were tired of period horror and familiar with traditional images of Dracula to the point of boredom.

Coppola saw *Bram Stoker's Dracula* as
a commercial proposition to pay off
debts and chose his cast of stars accordingly

stylised, non-realistic film

To attract the young audience who were the mainstay of the film industry in the 1990s, Coppola deliberately cast young attractive male and female actors – including, as Mina, Winona Ryder; and as Jonathan Harker, Keanu Reeves.

For Van Helsing, Dracula's nemesis, Coppola chose Anthony Hopkins who had been awarded an Academy Award the previous year for the role of Hannibal Lecter in *The Silence of the Lambs*. Hopkins's association with the horror genre, and his new status as an Oscar-winner, made him a desirable person to include in the film, attracting fans who had enjoyed his previous role. In addition, he would also bring a *gravitas* to the film.

For the role of Dracula, the British actor Gary Oldman was chosen. A 'method' actor, Oldman was already renowned for playing outsiders and 'dangerous' characters.

Coppola and Hart also realised that in order to be successful their film would have to differ from previous versions, and this they achieved in three ways: firstly they decided to introduce elements of the historical Dracula, Vlad Tepes, and when they discovered a story about his wife committing suicide in the mistaken belief that her husband had been killed by Turks they decided to use this as the basis of the film. Thus, *Dracula* would be the story of a man whose abiding passion is to search the centuries for his beloved wife, finally reincarnated in Mina more than 400 years later.

The fact that suicides are not able to enter Heaven gives Vlad the reason to disavow the Church, turn against Christ, and so provide a reason why the symbols of Christianity are so antagonistic to him. Hart's screenplay was the first to include Quincey Morris, Seward and Holmwood as the three suitors of Lucy.

Like *One from the Heart*, the film was to be made exclusively on the Sony sound stages in Hollywood, apart from one location scene – London, where Dracula meets Mina – which was shot on the Universal backlot. This allowed Coppola to have full control over the look of the film and to create the stylised, non-realistic film he wanted. Principal photography began on 14 October 1991. The cutting and editing were essentially computerised, with videotape replacing film so that rushes could be seen and managed more easily. Storyboards were created for around 1000 shots.

After previews in Seattle and San Rafael, compositional changes were made with Hopkins as Van Helsing narrating the film, linking past and present, which pleased the audience at a later preview in Denver. Because of the graphic violence and sex scenes, the film was given an R rating in the USA and an 18 certificate in the UK which would exclude much of the potential audience since the 15-24 age group contained the most prolific cinemagoers.

Nevertheless, the film became one of the most successful horror movies in history, grossing $82 million at the American box office and over $200 million worldwide. The first five days gross of $35 million was the largest in Columbia's history. Not only did the film justify Columbia's faith in Coppola and pay off his debts, but the film went on to win three Academy awards, for best make-up, sound-effects editing and costumes.

influences on production

DRACULA – THE STAGE PRODUCTION

Using the successful stage play rather than the original novel as its source, the film sticks very closely to the play as adapted for the American stage, helped by the casting of Bela Lugosi in the lead when Lon Chaney died. Lugosi's arrival made it unlikely and difficult to deviate too much from the stage version, other actors also reprising their stage roles. Thus, the sets are limited with entrances and exits coming from a few selected areas, and no location filming.

The ending of the film and the climax of the movie is the death of Dracula which happens off screen and is almost forgotten about as the attention is directed to Jonathan Harker's rescue of Mina. While, for reasons of space and difficulties of set-change, off-stage climax are common in the theatre, including Shakespeare, film is a supremely visual medium which demands the climax to be seen. For this reason modern audiences, having been brought up with these climactic endings in countless thrillers, Westerns and especially horror films, feel cheated.

BRAM STOKER'S DRACULA – THE NOVEL

By returning to the source of the character, Coppola felt able to dispense with previous images and create a character more in tune with Stoker's. At the same time, this enabled him to aim at a new audience who found no appeal in the traditional image. Not only did the novel's publication coincide with the beginnings of cinema, thus allowing Coppola to pay his homage, but the structure of the novel with its use of a variety of communication devices, and the historical setting at the end of one century and the beginning of another, was ideal in exploring one of Coppola's preoccupations: the meeting of the old and the new. Traditional ideas, as represented by superstition and Dracula, were replaced by science and reason in the form of Van Helsing, with women as one of the major battlegrounds.

technological advances

SOUND

At the beginning of the 1930s, many of the genres with which we have now become very familiar were in their early stages with conventions and stylistic features still not fully stabilised. Horror movies, like those of other genres, had existed in the days of the silent cinema but the arrival of sound had implications for plots, and style. Early cameras were noisy and ponderous and had very limited movement, unlike the silent era where cameras had become very fluid with much use of outdoor locations.

Sound also shifted the emphasis for carrying the narrative from the visuals to the dialogue. To make films more 'realistic' than silent ones, early sound films disposed of the accompanying incidental music, with the result that *Dracula* seems emotionally understated. Within a very short time, this was recognised and the musical soundtrack was reinstated.

Because the dialogue was pre-eminent and cameras had limited movement, shots tended to be static, often with long- or mid-shots of

technological advances

characters and limited use of close-ups. An additional factor was the Hollywood preoccupation with elocution. Early sound actors were often recruited from the stage, while others took elocution lessons in order to sound like stage actors whose clear articulated tones often seem too precise and slow to us, with the result that they appear to talk at length and interminably.

All these factors combined to remove the necessary pace of the movie. To modern audiences raised on steadicams and tracking shots the film lacks pace and is too wordy.

Unlike Browning, Coppola had available very sophisticated sound techniques which enabled him to record in stereo and utilise surrounding sound techniques to enhance the experience for the audience. As well as delivering a very loud, almost operatic score, he could create all sorts of sound effects to direct audience emotions and reactions.

GERMAN EXPRESSIONISM

One influence on horror movies in the silent era continued into sound. German expressionism was an artistic movement which sought to represent subjective experience through lighting and set design. Lighting made great use of shadows and clearly demarcated areas of light and shade. For a genre whose stock in trade is fear, shadows are an obvious way of creating suspense and tension and producing the appropriate mood.

Sets were designed to create odd angles and to be often non-realistic, recreating the world of nightmares. The combination of lighting and set design produced exactly the right atmosphere for many horror films, creating unease in the audience's minds.

Influences on the early Universal horror films, which included *Dracula*, were F.W. Murnau's *Nosferatu: A Symphony in Terror* and Pabst's *The Cabinet of Dr Caligari*. Many German film-makers had emigrated to the United States in the 1920s and brought their styles and influences with them. Obviously not all horror films use the extremes of German expressionism, but most of the period costume horrors, such as vampire and *Frankenstein* movies, reveal some influence whether through the lighting, sets or both.

As mentioned earlier, Universal was very familiar with the work of the leading expressionist practitioners and the effectiveness of their techniques. Coppola, too, utilised the ideas of the expressionists in creating appropriate moods and subjective reality in many of the scenes. As his film was made in colour, the adoption of tones to convey emotion and subjectivity is a feature of the cinematography of his film.

INTERTEXTUALITY

It would be unwise to forget Coppola's intention to celebrate 100 years of cinema with his film. This intention dominates the use of historical editing techniques, such as the iris and lap dissolves, as well as filling the screen with references to other films and directors.

The opening shots of the film, where Dracula, silhouetted against a scarlet sky, battles with the Turks, recall the work of German film animator Lotte Reiniger; while the battle scenes themselves are a deliberate homage to Kurasawa's film *Kagemusha* and Orson Welles's *Chimes at Midnight*.

Among other references to cinema history are Dracula's private chapel, with its icons and priestly robes reminiscent of Eisenstein's *Ivan the Terrible*, while inside the castle is a statue and torch which is a homage to Jean Cocteau's *La Belle et la bete* (*Beauty and the Beast*). In one scene where Dracula is entering the bedroom to attack Lucy, we see a shadow on the wall of her room of a long bony hand and arm stretching out towards her in a direct reference to Murnau's *Nosferatu*.

THE HORROR GENRE

The most obvious influence is probably the least: the demands of the genre itself. Since horror movies in the sound era had yet to develop and stabilise their features, rather than being tied to set conventions and expectations – apart from the obvious ones of creating fear and using shadows to create mood – it was *Dracula* which established the genre in the minds of the audiences and which became the template for future vampire films.

Coppola, on the other hand, not only had to find a new approach to a genre which seemed to have become moribund, but also had to ensure that audience expectations of the genre were fulfilled. Thus, we find familiar elements, such as expressionist lighting and storms to create atmosphere, interspersed with romantic interludes between Dracula and Mina. Coppola also had to contend with audience expectations from newer more explicit horror genres such as the slasher movie.

CONTINUITY EDITING

After taking into account all the above factors, it must be remembered that studios had begun to evolve a system of film-making which was quick and efficient and which used a limited number of techniques. This system became known as continuity editing after the most obvious stylistic feature, namely: establishing shot, shot and reverse shot. Other techniques to look for, include shallow focus, use of close-ups, use of lighting, use of dialogue, mise-en-scène, and how characters are arranged in the shot.

industrial context

UNIVERSAL STUDIOS

In the early 1930s Universal, which was founded in 1912 by Carl Laemmle Sr, was one of the poorest studios. But its decision to make horror movies introduced the modern horror genre to Hollywood. Heavily influenced by German film-makers and Expressionism, Universal had had connections with fantasy and horror since the 1920s, including *The Phantom of the Opera* (1925).

Among its top directors were Tod Browning and James Whale. Although their cycle of horror films were successful for the studio, by the middle of the 1930s the studio had serious financial problems which were only resolved by a series of musicals starring Deanna Durbin.

In 1962, Universal was acquired by MCA Inc., an entertainment conglomerate, and, since the 1970s, has enjoyed much success primarily through its association with Steven Spielberg, from *Jaws* (1975) to *ET: The Extra-Terrestrial* (1982) and *Jurassic Park* (1993). In 1990, Universal was acquired by Japan's Matsushita Electrical Industrial Company which purchased Universal's parent company, MCA Inc.

PRODUCT DIFFERENTIATION

The transition to sound and the drop in audiences caused by the Depression had caused financial problems for every studio. Many studios had filed for bankruptcy and financial restructuring led to many being controlled by Eastern banking corporations. This in turn forced studios to look for less riskier ways of achieving a return on investments.

Universal's response, like other studios, was to identify themselves with a particular genre. Genres were a surer guarantee of audiences and most of the key genres, such as musicals, Westerns, romantic comedies, became formalised at this time. Universal's strategy was to promote new stars, using their visually very striking new genre of horror. The films released at this time – and popular with audiences – belonged mainly to escapist genres like the ones mentioned above which allowed audiences to forget their troubles (see Social Context).

COLUMBIA PICTURES

Founded by Harry and Jack Cohen in 1920, the studio remained profitable through the Depression due to the leadership of Harry Cohen, and its policy of borrowing stars and directors from other studios thus avoiding the costs of stars' contracts. Bought by Coca-Cola in 1982 for $750 million, the studio was sold again in 1989 to the Sony Corporation of Japan for $3.4 million. Together with the production arm, TriStar Pictures, it forms Sony Pictures Entertainment.

TRISTAR PICTURES

Production and distribution company founded in 1982 by CBS, HBO (Home Box Office) and Columbia Pictures. The three companies represented television broadcasting, cable television and cinema distribution respectively. Within a few years Columbia became the major owner as CBS left and HBO reduced its share.

In 1987, TriStar merged with Columbia Pictures to form Columbia Pictures Entertainment. In 1989, Sony purchased both Columbia and TriStar which became self-contained financier-distributors under the aegis of Sony contexts **industrial context**

Pictures Entertainment. The company also distributes independent films by people such as Francis Ford Coppola and Woody Allen, as well as more mainstream films such as *Rambo* (1985), *Total Recall* (1990), *Terminator 2* (1991), and *Sleepless in Seattle* (1993).

AMERICAN ZOETROPE

In 1969, after receiving financial backing from Warner Bros., Francis Ford Coppola established American Zoetrope as a small production studio. Initially George Lucas was appointed vice-president but after only one film, Lucas's *THX 1138* Zoetrope found itself heavily in debt, a situation which was to recur. However successes, such as *The Godfather* turned round the situation.

In 1975, Coppola expanded American Zoetrope and took on loans to finance *Apocalypse Now!*. Although the costs escalated, the film was a critical and commercial success and partly solved his financial problems. Once again Coppola expanded the company into a full-scale production company, but the studio-bound, lavish, old-fashioned musical *One from The Heart* was a critical and commercial disaster. This was followed by *The Cotton Club*, another flop, and American Zoetrope filed for bankruptcy in 1990.

Although Coppola continued to make movies, they were on a smaller scale but were well received. By 1992, Coppola intended to make *Bram Stoker's Dracula*, a lavish big-budget movie to wipe out his debts and to show critics that he could make an expensive mainstream movie and complete it on schedule and on budget.

MULTI-MEDIA COMPANIES AND CAMPAIGNS

Like all major film studios, Columbia is part of a multi-media corporation which allows the film to be exploited through spin-off deals with other companies within the corporation. Eight *Dracula*-related books, including a lavish coffee-table book celebrating the costumes in the film, were released, a video game version, and a soundtrack album released by Columbia Records.

However, intended links with the American Red Cross for a blood-donors' drive, and with toy companies and fast-food chains, collapsed because of the film's erotic content and AIDS-related themes.

censorship & codes of conduct

The contrasting depiction of sex and violence marks the films as products of their particular times. For modern audiences, Tod Browning's film can seem 'tame', although some would say that its understated depiction of sexuality is more effective for being so. But to understand the way the films tackle these issues, one has to understand the codes of censorship that were in operation in each era.

In 1930, in response to public concern about the 'immorality' of the film industry, the Motion Picture Producers and Distributors of America (MPPDA) introduced a voluntary code of ethics which laid out what could or could not be shown in American movies. Although explicit scenes of violence were to be avoided (there is only one image of on-screen violence in *Dracula*, and even the traditional and generically obligatory bite-marks on the neck are hidden from the camera), the code was much stricter in matters of sex.

Among the regulations was one which referred to venereal diseases as not being suitable subjects for motion pictures. By 1934, the code was made mandatory. Obviously, with the relationship between vampirism, sexual immorality and venereal disease implied in the novel, the code posed problems for the film-makers.

But, as so often happened in movies of this time, film-makers circumvented the code through symbolism and subtle allusions, situations and dialogue with hidden meanings. So when Mina announces that she is a 'changed girl' and feels wonderful, the subtext is not hard to decipher. Harker may be puzzled when he says to Mina, 'Your eyes – they look at me so strangely' but we're not.

In 1968, a ratings system was introduced in the USA along the lines of the one which Great Britain had had for many years. This remains with a few

social context

alterations. *Bram Stoker's Dracula* was awarded an R rating (restricted) which meant that no children under the age of seventeen or eighteen, depending on State, could be admitted unless accompanied by a parent or adult guardian.

Censorship, however, has relaxed greatly in the last thirty years in the USA and this category is now the most common one for dealing with adult themes and allows quite explicit depictions of sex and violence. (There are two categories beyond this one: NC-17 – no children – and X which is reserved for pornographic films.) Thus, Coppola was not faced with the same restrictions as Browning and could make quite explicit the connections between sex, morality and disease. However, this does not necessarily make for a more effective film; in fact, commercial pressures often result in films being as explicit as they can in terms of the rating they desire.

social context

In 1929, the Wall Street Crash had ushered in the Great Depression, and the optimism and hedonism of the Roaring Twenties had given way to long unemployment queues. Realistic stories, which tried to address the problems of the time, were not popular. Audiences did not want to be reminded of their condition, they wanted to leave their troubles behind them at the cinema doors.

Escapist films, such as Westerns, murder mysteries, musical comedies including Marx Brothers films and romantic films about the rich, were what appealed to audiences. *Dracula* fitted into this fare, enabling audience's fears to be confronted and overcome on screen in a metaphorical form. Indeed, there is a good case to be made that since horror films are metaphors for our own fears and perform a mythic function they are more popular in times of trouble. For example, the science fiction/horror hybrids of the 1950s, arose out of concerns about the Cold War, nuclear weapons and its dangers of radiation.

Similarly, in 1992, the United States was experiencing a trade war with Japan, and growing unemployment. In both eras, as in the era of the novel – the 1890s – women were posing a threat to the patriarchal society of the bourgeoisie (see Ideology). But one fear dominates *Bram Stoker's Dracula* and was deliberately introduced into the film by Coppola and screenwriter James V. Hart: AIDS.

A disease of the blood that is primarily spread by sexual contact, both heterosexual and homosexual, AIDS is also seen as a 'foreign' disease due to research which speculates on its origins in Africa. This introduces a punishment for sexual promiscuity akin to syphilis in the nineteenth century. Vampirism is a metaphor for AIDS, and the disruption of family life and values caused by vampirism is symbolic of the effect of AIDS on society. This connection is made quite explicit in the film, even down to shots of blood cells co-mingling as Dracula bites Lucy and turns her into a vampire.

IDEOLOGY

This term is familiar to us from political parties, but the concept is much wider than that, describing a set of interlocking ideas, values and beliefs which can be held by individuals or groups within society. Ideology is often presented as 'natural' or 'self-evident' so that the beliefs are rarely questioned but taken for granted.

Ideology, which is defined as representing an entire society or country, actually emanates from particular social groups whose influence over affairs is greatest – 'the ruling classes'. The dissemination of their ideological beliefs as 'common sense' naturalises these beliefs, and enables the élite groups who run the country to continue to run it. This dominant ideology is disseminated through institutions such as the education system, the political system, and the mass media, including cinema.

Central to the ideological values of America, and Western Europe, is the family, and any danger to the country is often expressed in terms of the effect on the family. Morality is also a feature of ideological concerns in horror movies. Contemporary horror genres, such as the slasher movie, are often interpreted in terms of concerns about teenage morality with promiscuity being punished. This is particularly so of women, and similar concerns about women's sexuality and their role within society are expressed in both *Dracula* movies, irrespective of the sixty-year gap between them.

DRACULA AND THE 1930S

After the huge migrations from Europe to the United States, attitudes to immigration to the USA had hardened by the 1920s. It was believed that immigrants were taking jobs from American workers, and threatened the American way of life by bringing in un-American ideas, particularly Communism.

Also, by the early 1920s, feelings were running so strongly that Congress passed laws limiting the numbers of immigrants entering the country. This coincided with the revival of the Ku Klux Klan and took place at a time of great prosperity in the country – the so-called Roaring Twenties. However, in 1929, the stock market collapsed – the Wall Street Crash – ushering in the Great Depression.

By 1931, there were nearly eight-million Americans out of work, a figure which rose to nearly twenty-five per cent of the workforce by 1933. Just as with the original *Dracula* novel, a fear of foreigners and their effects on domestic society, is revealed in Browning's film, and expressed as an attack on the country's morals through an attack on women, as the main indicators of family.

Allied to this, is the position of women in the early 1930s. Again, just as the novel reflects fears of women's demands for emancipation at the end of the nineteenth century, so the film reflects the change in women's attitudes and social conditions since the end of the First World War when women found themselves performing jobs formerly reserved for men. The 1920s saw a new type of woman emerge – more assertive and independent and more sexually aware. By the end of the decade, women were fully emancipated, having been awarded the same voting rights as men.

The film reflects these social changes in the behaviour and aspirations of the women in the film. This change in women's roles was seen as a threat to the family. So the film reflects ideological concerns about how the changing roles of women would affect fundamental features of society, not only traditional family values but also power relations within a patriarchal society. In short, the emancipation of women was a threat to families, and males in general, and was caused in part by the influence of immigrants bringing in new ideas and morals to the United States.

This can be seen in the film when Lucy's conversion to vampire, obviously indicates a change in her morals thanks to the foreigner Dracula, and also with her attacks on children – the traditional heart of the family. The woman/mother-figure turning on her children is a powerful image of the destruction of traditional values.

BRAM STOKER'S DRACULA AND THE 1990S

Although sixty years later when, superficially, many changes have taken place in society, *Bram Stoker's Dracula* still exhibits ideological concerns in the same areas: the USA is still a society which both presents itself as the land of opportunity and also fears being swamped by immigrants, particularly those from Mexico, Latin America and the Far East. At a time of recession, like the 1930s, Americans resented foreigners arriving in their country, legally or illegally. Economically, the country was under threat from countries of the Pacific Rim.

As a result of these fears, in 1995 a bill was introduced into the House of Representatives reducing legal immigration from 800,000 a year to 500,000. Many Republicans did not support the bill, wanting all immigration stopped while there was unemployment in the United States.

The fear of immigrants was based on perceptions that they took jobs from Americans, as well as living off the State: in the early 1990s 6.6 per cent of foreign-born residents received welfare benefits compared to 4.9 per cent of native-born citizens. In addition, 25 per cent of prisoners were foreign-born.

Racial tensions also revealed themselves before and after the beating of Rodney King in March 1991 by Los Angeles police officers, and in the ensuing riots that followed the police officers' acquittal when fifty-three people died. This occasion also saw the rise of militias in various parts of the country – people, mainly white, dissatisfied with liberal attitudes to foreigners and with the United Nations which they saw as a threat to traditional American values, such as the rights of the individual and the right to carry guns.

Moreover, two years previously in the Gulf War the United States had led Coalition forces against an eastern tyrant – Saddam Hussein. It is, therefore, not difficult to see echoes of this in the film's ideology where another multi-national coalition, the Dutch Van Helsing, the American Morris and the English Harker, act against another eastern tyrant's aggression and expansionist policies.

Although, by 1992, women were playing a stronger role within US society, in many respects America was still a patriarchal society. Although women constituted 51 per cent of the population and 53 per cent of voters, they had only 13 per cent of members of Congress, 8 per cent of state governors, and 21 per cent of state legislators.

Furthermore, the traditional role of wife, mother and homemaker was still strong in many parts of the United States, and, while divorce was high, the family was still seen as the cornerstone of society. Once again, Lucy's attacks on babies is highlighted to indicate the threat to family values inherent in vampirism.

Undoubtedly, attitudes to sex have relaxed in the USA since the 1930s, as seen in the depiction of sex in the movies. However, the 'sexual liberation' of women, which began in the 1960s, could be seen – as it was in the 1930s – as a threat to the patriarchal US society.

The horror movie, with its sub-genre the slasher movie, could reflect this fear. In these films, sexually promiscuous women are punished by being murdered; and while the protagonist is often, if not usually, female, perhaps indicating their growing assertiveness, she is not sexually active. Instead, her virginity or celibacy is a confirmation of traditional American values.

In *Bram Stoker's Dracula*, as in the 1931 film, it is the sexually promiscuous women, like Lucy, who are turned into vampires or die, while less threatening women like Mina survive. In both films, the vampire and his vampire women are defeated through collective action by males. In both the 1890s and 1930s, vampirism is equated with sexual licence and thus with sexual diseases such as syphilis. In the 1990s, the disease equated with vampirism is AIDS.

REPRESENTATION OF WOMEN

In both films, dominant readings reflect a patriarchal view of society where women should remain in the domestic sphere. *Dracula*, in particular, demonstrates that women in films tend to have passive roles. Both Lucy and Mina are rather anodyne characters; even Lucy who is meant to be more sexually aware and adventurous is not seen in aggressive roles.

Even when she is a vampire, there are only glimpses of her and these tend to show her in a trance-like state, which is the fate of all the other women who cross Dracula's path. In this film, women are weak and ineffectual; even Mina's attempt to bite Harker's neck is half-hearted. It is men who are the active characters, influencing events and resolving problems while women are victims. Although women had been emancipated, the power still definitely lay with men, and when women stray from their assigned roles they are punished.

In *Bram Stoker's Dracula*, however, superficially the situation is the same but such a reading is more problematic. Mina is already an independent woman as she works as a schoolteacher, while both she and Lucy are the most sympathetic characters in the film. There is a liveliness about them which is missing from the men who are staid, stuffy and rather humourless.

Even though the men band together at the end to confront Dracula, it is Mina, now dying because of drinking Dracula's blood, who kills Dracula, causing his redemption to take place. As a result a more appropriate reading of the film is one which sees women as strong, independent characters repressed by a male-dominated society.

DRACULA – THE CHARACTER

The Dracula familiar to cinemagoers is not the creation of Bram Stoker, but of Hamilton Deane and John L. Balderston. Stoker's Dracula is not the elegant figure that has passed into popular imagination. Stoker's Dracula is a hairy-palmed, hoary-headed old Tartar whose bad breath and pointed ears make him an unlikely seducer. He is revolting.

While in *Bram Stoker's Dracula*, Dracula grows younger, he never grows attractive, although Coppola makes him so for the purposes of the love story and to increase the audience's sympathy for him. Browning, on the other hand, makes no effort to alter Dracula's appearance, preferring to depict him in a way in which his appearance and sexual magnetism are related to the persona of the Latin lover of the 1920s, Rudolph Valentino.

By drawing on a persona created on stage by Lugosi, Browning's Dracula is made to be sexually appealing to the audience. His actual appearance never changes, but this creates a problem since it tends to play down the sexual aggression and danger associated with Stoker's Dracula by emphasising his exotic nature and charisma. Coppola, however, utilises the vampire's ability to change shape to emphasise the human and non-human aspects of his nature.

All the key features of appearance that we have come to associate with Dracula were established in the Broadway play and by Lugosi: the full-dress evening clothes, the red-lined cape, the signet ring and the heavy distinctive Continental accent and delivery. Universal went with this representation since it had been successful in the theatre and would presumably be so in the film.

The original literary version did not hold enough appeal to make it a viable box-office proposition. Similar problems faced the 1992 version where over-familiarity with the Lugosi-inspired image had no box-office appeal left. A recourse to the historical inspiration allowed a more human, sympathetic, complex character to emerge that was more in tune with modern audiences raised on a diet of anti-heroes.

In keeping with Coppola and Hart's attempt to reinterpret Dracula (see Costume), Gary Oldman tried to bring a more human, sympathetic reading to the character while not losing any of Dracula's evil nature. In admitting that his accent owed everything to Lugosi, he also demonstrated the difficulty of completely diverging from existing representations. A criticism of Oldman is that he lacks a physical presence and, therefore, when out of make-up loses much of the character's threat. However, this does make him a more human, vulnerable Dracula, the first to cry on screen.

ATTITUDES TO CLASS

In the 1931 film, the working-class characters, the male nurse Martin and the maid, function as comic relief, particularly Martin. His walk is funny, his cap sits at an odd angle on his head and, like the maid, he speaks in what passes in Hollywood for a Cockney accent. All this contrasts with the middle-class characters who represent normality in their clothes, 'accentless' voices and behaviour. The representations reflect attitudes to class at a time when the lower classes knew their place, had limited social mobility, and no access to positions of power in both British and US society.

genre

Both films belong to the horror genre – more specifically the vampire movie sub-genre. Such a statement seems self-evident since genre identification is one of those skills that all movie audiences claim to have. However, a distance of sixty years separates the two films and fails to take account of the changes within the genre over those years. So, to call them 'typical' examples of horror films is an over-simplification.

Horror, more than other genres, has taken many forms over the years from Gothic horror to science fiction horror hybrids of the 1950s to contemporary slasher movies. At first glance, all these sub-genres seem to have little in common except intention – to induce fear in the audience. But, even here, this does not apply neatly to all modern horror films, where inducing revulsion is as much the intention as inducing fear. Also, modern audiences tend not to find Tod Browning's film remotely scary so that it fails even this rudimentary test.

All genres are not immutable but change over the years or go out of fashion. Genre has four functions:

- industrial
- audience
- mythic
- ideological.

For the film industry, genre films take some of the risk out of film-making by repeating previously successful formulas in the hope that the success will be repeated. For audiences, genre films also remove risk by giving cinemagoers an indication of what to expect and by allowing them to gain extra pleasure from the chance to demonstrate their generic competences.

Genre films also have a mythic function in that they provide simple solutions to problems, as well as an ideological function in that they reinforce existing dominant attitudes and beliefs due to the essentially conservative nature of genre.

Essentially, genre involves the repetition of a set of features from setting, character and plots to conventions and structures. However, problems can set in with a genre such as horror which has many sub-genres and whose visual features, such as setting, can alter drastically.

Different genres are often merged in one film. Is *The Rocky Horror Picture Show* a horror film or a musical? To answer this question, one should take Rick Altman's advice and examine the syntax or structure of the film as opposed to the semantics which refer to the visuals and sound elements of the film. In this case, a film like *The Rocky Horror Picture Show* belongs more properly to the musical since it is structured around the need to have songs and dances every so often. In addition, the film does not set out to scare so fails on this account as well.

However, a film such as *Star Wars* has borrowed its syntax from the Western, but it would be misleading to think of it as a Western since the semantics in this case take precedence with the audience. Also, narrative resolutions are often specific to particular genres: the musical likes to finish with a big set-piece song-and-dance number, while Westerns have a shoot-out either between individuals or between opposing groups such as the US cavalry and bands of Red Indians.

Horror, on the other hand, traditionally finishes with a confrontation between monster (and by monster I mean everything from vampires to creatures to human psychopaths in slasher movies). Freudians see this as the audience confronting its fears vicariously and learning how to cope with them.

Because the horror genre has so many variations, one has to look for common features in all the sub-genres; these are the presence of a monster (traditionally non-human but more recently very human); a protagonist who has to confront and defeat the monster; structure, as discussed earlier; resolution, in which the monster is defeated; and audience expectations, which refer to both the intention of the film in terms of scaring or revolting the audience, and also in allowing the audience to employ its generic knowledge.

An examination of the two *Dracula* films as examples of the horror genre reveals obvious similarities, but also significant differences. Since the subject-matter is the same, the films exhibit the same structures, characters and resolutions (with a significant difference). There are differences which include the treatment of Dracula's character, the display of violence and the depiction of sex, as well as the use of humour and its association with violence.

The differences between the films are due to technological advances which allow better, more realistic special effects and changing audience expectations.

In 1931, there were no supernatural horror movies and certainly no canon of vampire movies with which an audience could be familiar – therefore the expectations of the audience were quite different from those in 1992. By then, audiences were not only over-familiar – if not bored – with Dracula as a character and as a sub-genre, but had grown accustomed to changes within the horror genre as a whole. Such changes included more graphic violence, more overt and explicit connections of violence and sex, and humour associated with violent acts.

Humour – as a way of relieving tension, or catching the audience off-guard and thus unprepared for the next shock – has always had a role in horror. However, in more recent times, partly due to the audience's familiarity with the conventions of the genre, humour has been associated with the acts of violence themselves. This we see illustrated in *Bram Stoker's Dracula*, in the juxtaposition of the scene where Lucy as vampire is decapitated, her head spinning, blood-red against a black background, in stylised slow-motion, with a close-up of Van Helsing carving a bloody side of roast beef.

More importantly, perhaps, is the changing representation of Dracula himself and his metamorphosis into a more sympathetic character.

Because of the sixty-year gap between the two films it is difficult to see them as 'typical'. In 1931, there were no other comparable films other than possibly *Nosferatu* which had a different portrayal of Dracula. *Dracula* can only be seen as 'typical' in that it influenced the development of the Gothic horror movie and created an image of the vampire which dominated vampire films until the 1990s. If there is a 'typical' vampire film, then *Dracula* provides the type to be followed.

What of Coppola's film? Certainly, in terms of atmosphere and structure and resolution, it follows the conventions laid down by the earlier film, but it is atypical in terms of the portrayal of Dracula and the style of the film.

It is difficult to choose 'typical' films. Instead, a selection of vampire films will demonstrate the development of the vampire in film.

Nosferatu: A Symphony in Terror (1922). Murnau's film was an unauthorised adaptation of Stoker's novel, but it retains a power that few silent films have, and the depiction of Count Orlok (Dracula) as a repulsive rodent-like creature with two central fangs is closer to Stoker's original. There is no sexual allure, but the association of vampirism with plague and disease is made very clearly. It had a huge stylistic influence, but, while remaining the scariest vampire ever to appear on screen, the depiction of the vampire had no commercial appeal.

Dracula (in USA full title *The Horror of Dracula*, 1958). Hammer Films' version revitalised the genre and created another star in Christopher Lee whose Dracula is arguably as famous as Lugosi's, whose costume he borrowed. Lee's was a more overtly sexual and animal-like Dracula, full of pent-up aggression and sexual tension.

Hammer's film and its sequels brought the sexual elements to the fore, partly through Lee, but also through the films' emphasis on blood and gore and scantily-clad female victims, all filmed in lurid colour. It is arguably as influential as Browning's film.

Near Dark (1987). Katherine Bigelow's film transported the vampire to modern mid-Western America, where a band of hillbilly outsiders roam the Midwest.

The Lost Boys (1987). Joel Schumacher's film aims directly at the teen audience. It cleverly used its audience's familiarity with the genre to mock the conventions which indicated the difficulties of making a straightforward traditional version of the Dracula story. A variation of Peter Pan has the vampires as restless teenage gang members. The knowledge to defeat them comes from comic books. This film and Bigelow's were indicative of a more sympathetic approach to vampires – an approach taken up by Coppola and then Neil Jordan in the film below.

Interview with the Vampire (1994) portrayed vampires as decadent and homoerotic. The vampires are not so much to be feared as pitied. Eternal life was never so boring.

AUDIENCE

As stated earlier, audiences help construct genres through their expectations. There are two ways of looking at audiences: as passive, where they receive information from the text on the screen in a one-way process, without contributing anything themselves. As active, where they actively construct meaning, rather than meaning simply being given to them, due to their own set of competences which include age, sex, social and cultural backgrounds, and also their pre-existing generic and filmic knowledge.

Therefore, instead of an audience being considered as one mass which interprets films in the same way, audiences are now seen as individuals who construct individual meanings according to the factors mentioned above. This is not to say that each person will interpret a film differently, but that the potential to do so is there.

Originally film audiences were seen as one mass to be attracted, but, within the last twenty to thirty years, they have become increasingly fragmented. Instead of aiming specifically at a mass audience, film studios now aim at niche audiences. Of course, mass audiences are important, and the bigger a movie's budget the more likely it is to appeal to a mass audience. However, rather than seeing this audience as one amorphous group, the industry splits it up into smaller groups.

Whereas in 1931, the audience would not be fragmented other than appealing in particular to females – as can be seen in the tagline for the film, 'The story of the strangest passion the world has ever known!' – by

filmography

1992 with fragmentation of the audience as an established feature of the industry, the film would be aimed at niche groups, but as many as possible.

Again, women would be targeted – particularly those between the ages of eighteen and thirty-five as the demographics of film-going in the late twentieth century had this age group as the most likely to go to the cinema. Again, the marketing for *Bram Stoker's Dracula* emphasised the sexual/romantic elements, this time with the tagline 'Love never Dies'.

The targeting would be done through casting stars in the eighteen to thirty-five age group who would be popular with the audience. However, fans of the horror-movie genre would be attracted, too. And this would be emphasised by the inclusion of Anthony Hopkins in the film because of his performance in the horror film *The Silence of the Lambs*.

filmography

TOD BROWNING

Surprisingly, Browning is best known today for a film which, until relatively recently, was rarely seen and which Browning himself withdrew after complaints and much controversy. *Freaks* (1932) is one of the most notorious films in movie history, and Browning never recovered from the furore caused by its release. A truly disturbing, unique movie, utilising Browning's own side-show experiences, the cast was mainly composed of real-life side-show freaks who, although treated with sympathy in the film by Browning, proved too much for audiences. A genuinely moving, disturbing movie.

FRANCIS FORD COPPOLA

Coppola's first movie, *Dementia 13* (1963), is a gory horror and is mentioned only to show the influence of Roger Corman.

The Godfather (1972) and *The Godfather Part II* (1974) are still two of cinema's great movies, demonstrating Coppola's command of narrative and style, as well as themes such as sympathy for outsiders and the meeting of old worlds with the new.

The Conversation (1974) and *Apocalypse Now!* (1979) both use the thematic device of the quest to structure the films, while *Apocalypse Now!* features some visually striking set pieces, perhaps indicating Coppola's future direction of style over content.

One for the Heart (1982), *Rumble Fish* (1983) and *The Outsiders* (1983) are noted more for their striking visual styles masking weak or thin narratives.

critical responses

Traditionally, there has been a dichotomy between the response of audiences and critics. Horror films have remained consistently popular with audiences over the decades while film critics have disparaged them. The release of *Dracula* in 1931 was generally well-received, with the *New York Times*'s review being typical:

> What with Mr. Browning's imaginative direction and Mr. Lugosi's make-up and weird gestures, this picture succeeds to some extent in its grand guignol intentions ... this picture can at least boast of being the best of the many mystery films.

There is no mention of it being a horror movie, indicative perhaps of its place at the beginning of the genre. Critics saw it belonging to a type of film known as the mystery genre, which covered previous horror movies which lacked a supernatural element. The *New York Daily News* also alludes to the film as a mystery:

> It is superbly photographed, and presented to audible screen audiences at the capable movie direction of Tod Browning – megaphone of so many mysteries that he knows every trick of the type. Carl Laemmle Jr counts Dracula among his productions for the season, and the boy's done well again. He chose director, cast and story wisely. Bela Lugosi's performance as Count Dracula is a repetition of his stage role. He's simply grand.

Many other reviews, such as that of the *Herald Tribune*, also singled out Lugosi's performance as the outstanding feature of the film:

critical responses

> Lugosi's performance is even more effective than he was on the stage, which is something of a tribute.

Sixty years later, the reviews for *Bram Stoker's Dracula* were more mixed. Advance publicity, emphasising the film's faithfulness to the novel and Coppola's reputation as an important film-maker, seemed to have created expectations which were not fulfilled. Many critics felt that the love story, created by Hart and Coppola, took liberties with the faithfulness; while others found fault with the acting, particularly that of Keanu Reeves who had struggled with the accent. Coppola was also criticised for producing a film that was a triumph of style over substance.

'Yes, the movie is lovingly shot with beautiful cinematography, lavish, elegant costuming, lush sets and excellent performances from Gary Oldman, Anthony Hopkins, and Winona Ryder ... But it's too long on style and illusionary effects and very short on substance,' commented Dolores Barclay of Associated Press.

Pam Cook, writing in *Sight and Sound* (February 1992), was critical of the film-makers' so-called faithful approach: '... authenticity was evidently the last thing on the film makers' minds'.

Like the 1931 film, the actor playing the Count is singled out. Gary Oldman's performance is received reasonably favourably, but the changes he undergoes in the film prevent him creating an effective persona as Lugosi did. As Angie Errigo, *Empire*, February 1992, says:

> Gary Oldman threatens to compel as the wrathful 15th century Transylvanian knight Vlad Dracula ... he is kept too busy to do so, though, transmogrifying into a repellent randy baboon, a slimy green bat thing, a green mist or, most alarmingly, so coiffeured and pancaked as Harker's host at Castle Dracula as to recall Alistair Sim in drag.

Angie Errigo's final comment sums up the difference in the reviews of the two films: in 1931, *Dracula* was truly an original movie, while in 1992 Coppola had to produce another original interpretation while still 'blood-drenched to terrific effect'

conforming to the expectations created by the 1931 film, Bela Lugosi and the other 160-plus vampire films.

As horror this is blood-drenched to terrific effect while never attaining the eeriness of Murnau's Nosferatu, the hypnotic perversion of Herzog's version or the ominous mood of Browning's Bela Lugosi evergreen. As a Gothic romance-let-rip, though, it is a thrill-seeker's rollercoaster ride.

bibliography

general film

Altman, Rick, *Film Genre*,
BFI, 1999
   Detailed exploration of film genres

Bordwell, David, *Narration in the
Fiction Film*, Routledge, 1985
   A detailed study of narrative theory
   and structures

– – –, Staiger, Janet & Thompson,
Kristin, *The Classical Hollywood
Cinema: Film Style & Mode of
Production to 1960*, Routledge, 1985;
pbk 1995
   An authoritative study of cinema as
   institution, it covers film style and
   production

– – – & Thompson, Kristin, *Film Art*,
McGraw-Hill, 4th edn, 1993
   An introduction to film aesthetics for
   the non-specialist

Branson, Gill & Stafford, Roy, *The
Media Studies Handbook*, Routledge,
1996

Buckland, Warren, *Teach Yourself
Film Studies*, Hodder & Stoughton,
1998
   Very accessible, it gives an overview of
   key areas in film studies

Cook, Pam (ed.), *The Cinema Book*,
BFI, 1994

Corrigan, Tim, *A Short Guide To
Writing About Film*,
HarperCollins, 1994
   What it says: a practical guide for
   students

Dyer, Richard, *Stars*, BFI, 1979;
pbk Indiana University Press, 1998
   A good introduction to the star
   system

Easthope, Antony, *Classical Film
Theory*, Longman, 1993
   A clear overview of recent writing
   about film theory

Hayward, Susan, *Key Concepts in
Cinema Studies*,
Routledge, 1996

Hill, John & Gibson, Pamela Church
(eds), *The Oxford Guide to Film Studies*,
Oxford University Press, 1998
   Wide-ranging standard guide

Lapsley, Robert & Westlake, Michael,
Film Theory: An Introduction,
Manchester University Press, 1994

Maltby, Richard & Craven, Ian,
Hollywood Cinema,
Blackwell, 1995
   A comprehensive work on the
   Hollywood industry and its
   products

Mulvey, Laura, 'Visual Pleasure and
Narrative Cinema' (1974), in *Visual
and Other Pleasures*,
Indiana University Press, Bloomington,
1989
   The classic analysis of 'the look' and
   'the male gaze' in Hollywood cinema.
   Also available in numerous other
   edited collections

Nelmes, Jill (ed.),
Introduction to Film Studies,
Routledge, 1996
   Deals with several national cinemas
   and key concepts in film study

Nowell-Smith, Geoffrey (ed.),
The Oxford History of World Cinema,
Oxford University Press, 1996
   Hugely detailed and wide-ranging
   with many features on 'stars'

Thomson, David, *A Biographical Dictionary of the Cinema*, Secker & Warburg, 1975
  Unashamedly driven by personal taste, but often stimulating

Truffaut, François, *Hitchcock*, Simon & Schuster, 1966, rev. edn, Touchstone, 1985
  Landmark extended interview

Turner, Graeme, *Film as Social Practice*, 2nd edn, Routledge, 1993
  Chapter four, 'Film Narrative', discusses structuralist theories of narrative

Wollen, Peter, *Signs and Meaning in the Cinema*, Viking, 1972
  An important study in semiology

Readers should also explore the many relevant websites and journals. *Film Education* and *Sight and Sound* are standard reading.

Valuable websites include:

The Internet Movie Database at
http://uk.imdb.com

Screensite at
http://www.tcf.ua.edu/screensite/contents.html

The Media and Communications Site at the University of Aberystwyth at
http://www.aber.ac.uk/~dgc/welcome.html

There are obviously many other university and studio websites which are worth exploring in relation to film studies.

dracula

Carroll, Noel, 'Notes on Dreyer's Vampyr' (essay) from *Interpreting the Moving Image*, Cambridge University Press, 1998

Coppola, Francis Ford, and Hart, James V., *Bram Stoker's Dracula: The Film and the Legend*, Newmarket Press, New York, 1992

Cowie, Peter, *Coppola*, Faber and Faber, London, 1998

Mark Jancovich, *Horror*, Batsford, London, 1992

Madison, Bob (ed.), *Dracula: the First Hundred Years*, Midnight Marquee Press Inc., Baltimore, 1997

Silver, Alain, and Ursini, James, *The Vampire Film*, Limelight Editions, Third edition, New York, 1997

Svelha, Gary J. and Susan (eds), *Bitches, Bimbos and Virgins: Women in the Horror Film*, Midnight Marquee Press Inc., Baltimore, 1996

Twitchell, James B., *Dreadful Pleasures: An Anatomy of Modern Horror*, Oxford University Press, 1985

cinematic terms

canted shots a shot where the camera is tilted off the horizontal

classical narration the dominant form of film-making between 1930 and 1960, emphasising story-telling and plot over style

continuity editing unobtrusive editing designed to move from shot to shot without drawing attention to itself

diegetic describes the fictional world of the film's narrative (diegesis)

establishing shot a feature of continuity editing where a long shot establishes place and/or character before cutting to closer shots

intercutting cutting between two shots or sequences in order to invite comparison and/or to indicate events happening simultaneously

iris an edit common in silent cinema where a fade in or out is done in a circular manner

lap dissolves an abbreviation for overlapping dissolves where one shot fades in, overlapping with another fading out

match on action a cut between two shots over which an action appears to continue smoothly

mythic, myth refers to any stories that try to explain a culture's basic beliefs about itself

POV a shot intended to be seen through the eyes or from the point of view of a particular character

process shot special effects shot in which live action is filmed in front of an image projected on to a screen from the rear

slasher movies sub-genre of horror in which people are pursued and killed by a psychopath wielding a knife or other sharp implement

steadicam trade name for a device which allows a hand-held camera to move smoothly and fluently

tagline the slogan used to advertise a film

tones tone refers to when one shade of colour dominates a scene

tracking shot when a camera is filming while being pushed along tracks or rails

vertical integration a term used to describe a film studio's control of the means of production, distribution and exhibition

voice-over (VO) speech that does not originate from the scene on film, but is superimposed over it

credits

dracula

production company
Universal

director
Tod Browning

producer
Carl Laemmle Jr.
A Tod Browning Production
presented by Carl Laemmle

book
Bram Stoker

adapted from the play by
Hamilton Deane and
John L. Balderston

play script
Garrett Fort

scenario supervision
Charles A. Logue

art director
Charles D. Hall

cinematographer
Karl Freund

editor
Milton Carruth

set designers
Herman Rosse, John Hoffman

photographic effects
Frank J. Booth

cast
Count Dracula – Bela Lugosi
Mina – Helen Chandler
Renfield – Dwight Frye
Van Helsing – Edward van Sloan
Dr Seward – Herbert Blundstone
Lucy – Frances Dade

bram stoker's dracula

distributor
Columbia TriStar

production company
American Zoetrope/
Osiris Films
For Columbia Pictures

executive producers
Michael Apted

Robert O'Connor

producers
Francis Ford Coppola
Fred Fuchs
Charles Mulvehill

co-producers
James V. Hart
John Veitch

associate producer
Susan Landau

2nd unit director
Roman Coppola

casting
Victoria Thomas

screenplay
James V. Hart

director of photography
Michael Ballhaus

colour
Technicolor

visual effects
Roman Coppola

editors
Nicholas C. Smith
Glen Scantlebury
Anne Goursaud

production designer
Thomas Sanders

music
Wojciech Kilar

music performed by
Los Angeles Master Chorale
Vocal: Diamanda Galás

cast
Count Dracula – Gary Oldman
Mina Murray/Elisabeta – Winona Ryder
Professor Abraham Van Helsing – Anthony Hopkins
Jonathan Harker – Keanu Reeves
Doctor Jack Seward – Richard E. Grant
Lord Arthur Holmwood – Cary Elwes
Quincey P. Morris – Bill Campbell
Lucy Westenra – Sadie Frost
R. M. Renfield – Tom Waits
Dracula's Brides – Monica Bellucci
Michaela Bercu
Florina Kendrick

Other titles in the series

Other titles available in the York Film Notes series:

Title	ISBN
8½ (Otto e mezzo)	0582 40488 6
A bout de souffle	0582 43182 4
Apocalypse Now	0582 43183 2
Battleship Potemkin	0582 40490 8
Blade Runner	0582 43198 0
Casablanca	0582 43200 6
Chinatown	0582 43199 9
Citizen Kane	0582 40493 2
Das Cabinet des Dr Caligari	0582 40494 0
Double Indemnity	0582 43196 4
Easy Rider	0582 43195 6
Fargo	0582 43193 X
Fear Eats The Soul	0582 43224 3
La Haine	0582 43194 8
Lawrence of Arabia	0582 43192 1
Psycho	0582 43191 3
Pulp Fiction	0582 40510 6
Romeo and Juliet	0582 43189 1
Some Like It Hot	0582 40503 3
Stagecoach	0582 43187 5
Taxi Driver	0582 40506 8
The Full Monty	0582 43181 6
The Godfather	0582 43188 3
The Piano	0582 43190 5
The Searchers	0582 40510 6
The Terminator	0582 43186 7
The Third Man	0582 40511 4
Thelma and Louise	0582 43184 0
Unforgiven	0582 43185 9

Also from York Notes

Also available in the **York Notes** range:

York Notes

The ultimate literature guides for GCSE students (or equivalent levels)

York Notes Advanced

Literature guides for A-level and undergraduate students (or equivalent levels)

York Personal Tutors

Personal tutoring on essential GCSE English and Maths topics

Available from good bookshops.

For full details, please visit our website at www.longman-yorknotes.com

notes

DRACULA

notes

notes

notes

notes

DRACULA